西北工业大学哲学社会科学繁荣发展计划精品专著

应用型文本翻译的理论与实践

刘美岩 编著

西北工业大学出版社

西 安

【内容简介】 本书首先介绍了德国功能学派翻译理论,其中包括莱斯的功能分类批评理论、弗米尔的目的论、曼塔丽的翻译行为理论和诺德的功能加忠诚理论;其次通过英汉对比,为两种语言的转换提供了参考;最后结合案例,分析了功能学派翻译理论对应用文翻译的指导意义,并总结了旅游文本、新闻报导、商务英语以及美术评述的翻译策略和方法。

本书既适合高校英语专业学生及对翻译感兴趣的读者阅读,也可供相关领域的工作人员学习参考。

图书在版编目(CIP)数据

应用型文本翻译的理论与实践 / 刘美岩编著. — 西安:西北工业大学出版社,2024.2
ISBN 978-7-5612-9214-3

Ⅰ.①应… Ⅱ.①刘… Ⅲ.①英语-翻译-研究 Ⅳ.①H315.9

中国国家版本馆 CIP 数据核字(2024)第 058982 号

YINGYONGXING WENBEN FANYI DE LILUN YU SHIJIAN
应 用 型 文 本 翻 译 的 理 论 与 实 践
刘美岩　编著

责任编辑:隋秀娟　李　欣	策划编辑:蒋民昌
责任校对:万灵芝	装帧设计:董晓伟

出版发行:西北工业大学出版社
通信地址:西安市友谊西路127号　　邮编:710072
电　　话:(029)88491757,88493844
网　　址:www.nwpup.com
印　刷　者:兴平市博闻印务有限公司
开　　本:787 mm×1 092 mm　　1/16
印　　张:9.25
字　　数:243 千字
版　　次:2024 年 2 月第 1 版　　2024 年 2 月第 1 次印刷
书　　号:ISBN 978-7-5612-9214-3
定　　价:55.00 元

如有印装问题请与出版社联系调换

Preface

In recent years, with the globalization of the economy and frequent international exchange in many fields, translation has become a booming industry. The focus of translation research has shifted from traditional literature translation to practical areas such as politics, economics, science and culture.

Since practical translation involves different types of text with different purposes, there is a great need to adopt proper translation strategies and methods with the instruction of proper theory. This is just what this book is concerned about.

The book consists of six chapters. The first chapter gives an introduction to the German school of functionalist translation theories from its four representatives' contributions: Reiss's Text Typology Theory, Vermeer's Skopos Theory, Manttari's Translational Action Theory, and Nord's Function Plus Loyalty Theory, which would shed light on different types of practical translation. The second chapter is devoted to the comparison and contrast between English and Chinese language, because a thorough understanding of the special features of the two languages can facilitate language conversion. The remaining four chapters elaborate on tourism translation, news report translation, business translation and fine art commentary translation respectively. Each chapter begins with an analysis of text features and translation purpose, followed by the guiding translation principles and translation strategies with many typical examples to fully illustrate the translation methods.

This book is based on the latest translation studies and researches both at home and abroad. It is specially designed for advanced English learners, translators, college English teachers and those who are interested in translation. It aims to provide readers with theoretical and practical guidance in practical translation.

Finally, the authors want to show their sincere gratitude and appreciations to Northwestern Polytechnical University for sponsoring the writing and publishing of this book.

Liu Meiyan
December, 2022

Contents

Chapter One Functionalist Translation Theories ……………………………………… 1

1.1 Background of Functionalist Translation Theories ……………………………… 1
1.2 Reiss's Text Typology Theory ……………………………………………………… 2
1.3 Vermeer's Skopos Theory …………………………………………………………… 4
1.4 Manttari's Translational Action Theory …………………………………………… 7
1.5 Nord's Function Plus Loyalty Theory ……………………………………………… 8
1.6 Newmark's Text Typology Theory ………………………………………………… 11
1.7 Significance of Functionalist Translation Theory ………………………………… 15

Chapter Two Contrastive Study Between English and Chinese ……………… 17

2.1 Differences in Word Order ………………………………………………………… 17
2.2 Hypotaxis of English vs. Parataxis of Chinese …………………………………… 23
2.3 English Subject-Predicate Structure vs. Chinese Topic-Comment Structure …… 26
2.4 Differences in Reference …………………………………………………………… 28
2.5 Nominalization of English Language and Its Translation ………………………… 30
2.6 English Passive Voice and Its Translation ………………………………………… 34

Chapter Three Translation of Tourism Promotional Texts …………………… 39

3.1 Definition of Tourism Promotional Texts ………………………………………… 39
3.2 Functions of the TPTs ……………………………………………………………… 40
3.3 Differences Between English and Chinese TPTs ………………………………… 40
3.4 Principles for Tourism Translation ………………………………………………… 48
3.5 Functional Approach in TPTs Translation ………………………………………… 49
3.6 C-E Translation of TPTs under the Guidance of Functional Approach ………… 50
3.7 E-C Translation of TPTs under the Guidance of Functional Approach ………… 60

Chapter Four Translation of News Report ………………………………………… 65

4.1 Relevant Concepts of News Report ………………………………………………… 65
4.2 Characteristics of News Language ………………………………………………… 66

4.3　Criteria and Principles for News Report Translation …… 74
4.4　Translation of News Headlines …… 76
4.5　Translation of News Lead …… 89

Chapter Five　Business English Translation …… 97

5.1　Definition of Business English …… 97
5.2　Linguistic and Stylistic Features of Business English …… 97
5.3　Contract Translation …… 105
5.4　Business Letter Translation …… 115

Chapter Six　C-E Translation of Fine Art Commentary …… 124

6.1　Functions of the Target Text …… 125
6.2　Linguistic Features of the Source Text …… 125
6.3　Criteria for Art Text Translation …… 127
6.4　Translation Methods of Fine Art Commentary …… 127

References …… 139

Chapter One   Functionalist Translation Theories

1.1 Background of Functionalist Translation Theories

As a popular translation theory, the functionalism did not appear overnight. It evolved from previous translation studies. Many literary and Bible translators have felt that the process of translating should involve both procedure: a faithful reproduction of formal source text qualities in one situation and adjustment to the target audience in another (Nord, 2001: 4). Similarly, Eugene A. Nida, a famous American translation theorist, distinguishes two types of equivalence in *Toward a Science of Translating* (1964) : formal equivalence and dynamic equivalence. In Nida's perspective, formal equivalence "focuses action on the message itself, in both form and content", while dynamic equivalence is based upon "the principle of equivalence effect" (Nida, 1964:159). He also pointed out that there is a priority of contextual consistency over verbal consistency and a priority of dynamic equivalence over formal correspondence.

When discussing the nature of translation, Nida defined that "translating consists in reproducing in the receptor language the closest natural equivalent of the source-language message" (Nida & Taber, 2007: 12) and emphasized that equivalence should be realized "in terms of the degree to which the receptors of the message in the receptor language respond to it in substantially the same manner as the receptors in the source language" (Nida & Taber, 2007: 24). As a result, when determining whether a translating work is faithful to the original text or not, critics should put the "receptors' response" rather than the formal structures between the source text and its translation as the first concern. This view is different from the traditional ones in which translation is mainly message-oriented. Later, in Nida's *From one Language to Another* (1986, with De Waard), the expression "dynamic equivalence" is replaced by "functional equivalence". But essentially there is not much difference between the two.

In "A Framework for the Analysis and Evaluation of Theories of Translation" , Nida (1976) places special emphasis on the purpose of the translation on the role of both the translator and the receiver, and on the cultural implication of the transition process:

The *relative adequacy of different translations of the same text can only be determined in terms of the extent to which each transition successfully fulfill the purpose for which it was intended* (1976).

To sum up, Nida's theory shifts the emphasis from the "verbal correspondence" to "functional equivalence", from "source text" to "readers' response" and "effect communication", which has widened the theoretical research angle and completely changed the situation of the static aspect of traditional translation mode, thus enables us to treat translating in a broad sense and laid the basis upon which a new field of investigation in the 20th century: the "science of translation" was founded (Nord, 2001).

However, Equivalence Theory has some limitations. First, equivalence can hardly be obtained in translation across cultures and languages, and it may not even be a desirable goal (Nord, 2001). There may be many cases of non-equivalence in translation caused by the pragmatic differences between source and target culture. Second, equivalence approach lacks consistency: some scholars regard literalism as the optimum procedure in translation (Newmark, 1984: 16); others such as Koller (1993: 53), allow a certain number of adaptive procedure, paraphrasing or other non-literal procedures in specific cases where they are intended to convey implicit source text values or to improve the comprehensibility of the text for the target audience. Different or even contradictory standards for the selection of transfer procedures are set up for different learners or text types. This makes the equivalence approach rather confusing. Therefore, we can see a shift from an overall focus on equivalence to the functional approach to translation in the new era.

Functionalist translation theories advanced in Germany in the 1970s and 1980s which moved translation from a mainly linguistic phenomenon to an act of intercultural communication. Its formation and development went through four main stages. The representatives are Katharina Reiss, Hans J. Vermeer, Justa Holz-Manttari and Christian Nord.

Reiss was the first person who links translation strategies with language function and text type. Her approach was later coupled to Vermeer's highly influential Skopos theory, where the translation strategy is decided by the purpose of the translation. Holz-Manttari proposed the concept of translation action that places professional translation within a sociocultural context and viewed translation as a communicative transaction involving initiator, commissioner, the producers, users and receivers of the source text (ST) and target text (TT). Nord's model, Functionality Plus Loyalty, is a supplement and further development of the functionalist translation theory.

1.2 Reiss's Text Typology Theory

Katharina Reiss, one of the representatives of German functionalist school, published a book *The Limitations and Possibilities of Translation Criticism* in 1971, which marked the establishment of functionalist translation theory. Reiss is the first person relating function

Chapter One Functionalist Translation Theories

with translation and distinguishing different text types.

Based on Karl Buhler's model of language functions, Reiss put forward translation-oriented text typology theory during the period of 1968 to 1969. In her paper "Text types translation types and translation assessment", she divided all texts into three main types, namely, content-focused text (informative text), form-focused text (expressive text) and appeal-focused text (operative text). She (2001:26) summarized the function of each type of text and gave suggestions on related translation methods as Table 1 shows:

Table 1 Text Types and Related Translation Methods

Text Type	Informative	Expressive	Operative
language function	representing objects and facts	expressing sender's attitude	making an appeal to text receiver
language dimension	logical	aesthetic	dialogic
text focus	content-focused	form-focused	appellative-focused
TT should…	transmit referential content	transmit aesthetic form	elicit desired response
translation method	"plain prose" explication as required	"identifying" method, adopt perspective of ST author	"adaptive", equivalent effect

Among the above three types, the principal function of an informative text is to convey information to the receiver, so its language is usually plain and logical with the content or "topic" as the focus of the communication. When translating such text, translators often adopt literal translation method. An expressive text is concerned with aesthetic value, and its informative aspect is partly complemented or even overruled by an aesthetic component. Therefore, the translator should give importance to produce an analogous aesthetic effect as well as the semantic content of the original. An operative text is appellative-focused with the purpose of activating action or persuading readers to do something. Translating this kind of text, translators should pay special attention to its persuasive effect by adopting flexible methods such as adaptation and paraphrasing.

Reiss (1988) stresses that the three categories cover all written texts, though some texts are compound texts, i.e. texts with more than one function. Indeed, many texts have multiple functions, primary or subordinate. The primary function of ST decides the translation method (Reiss, 1988:70). She also pointed out that translators and translation critics should analyze language features and functions as well as the forms of language expression in different types of text, which is the basis for translation and evaluation.

Munday (2001:76) points out that "the significance of Reiss's theory is that it broadens people's view to communicative purpose of translating beyond the linguistic level and the literal meaning. Nord (1997:9) regards Reiss' text typology as a "milestone", breaking through the shackles of traditional translation theory, which regards equivalence of words, sentences as the research basis and pushing the boundaries of Nida's concept of dynamic equivalence to new levels of flexibility and adaptability. Reiss's theory laid a solid foundation for the development of Skopos Theory.

1.3 Vermeer's Skopos Theory

In his book *A Framework for a General Theory of Translation* published in 1978, Hans J. Vermeer first put forward Skopos Theory (Skopostheorie), and introduced it in detail in the book *Groundwork for a General Theory of Translation*, which is co-authored with his teacher Reiss in 1984.

Skopos is a Greek word for "purpose". According to Skopostheorie, the prime principle determining any translation process is the purpose (Skopos) of the overall translational action. Apart from the term Skopos, Vermeer (1990:93) uses the related words "aim", "purpose", "intention" and "function". As a general rule he considers the teleological concepts aim, purpose, intention and function to be equivalent (Reiss and Vermeer, 1984: 96), subsuming them under the generic concept of Skopos.

Vermeer (1989a:100) distinguished three possible kinds of purpose in the field of translation: the general purpose aimed at by the translator in the translation process (perhaps "to earn a living"), the communicative purpose aimed at by the target text in the target situation (perhaps "to instruct the reader") and the purpose aimed at by a particular translation strategy or procedure (for example, "to translate literally in order to show the structural particularities of the source language"). Nevertheless, the term Skopos usually refers to the purpose of the target text.

According to Skopostheorie, another most important factor determining the purpose of a translation is the addressee, who is the intended receiver or audience of the target text with their culture-specific world-knowledge, their expectations and their communicative needs. Every translation is directed at an intended audience, since to translate means "to produce a text in a target setting for a target purpose and target addressees in target circumstances" (Vermeer, 1989a: 29).

In the case of a translation, the translator is a real receiver of the source text who then proceeds to inform another audience, located in a situation under target culture conditions, about the offer of information made by the source text.

1.3.1 Skopos rule

In Skopostheorie, the supreme guideline is "the Skopos rule", whatever type of translation it is. According to this rule, the translational action is decided by the purpose of the action:

Chapter One Functionalist Translation Theories

Every text is produced for, and hence serves a certain aim. Thus, the Skopos rule means: translating, explaining, reading or writing should follow a certain model, which enables the text/version to function in a certain situation. The text/version is intended for potential users and should function exactly as they expect (Vermeer, 1989a: 20).

The Skopos rule specifies that the translator must translate consciously and persistently in conformance with particular principles related to the target text. The Skopostheorie does not specify what the principles are; it depends on specific situations (Vermeer, 1989b: 182). Therefore, the top-ranking rule for any translation is thus the "Skopos rule", which says that a translational action is determined by its Skopos; that is, "the end justifies the means" (Reiss & Vermeer, 1984: 101).

However, most translational actions allow a variety of Skopos, which may be related to each other in a hierarchical order. Now the question is who decides what the purpose is. Since the translation is normally done "by assignment". A client needs a text for a particular purpose and calls upon the translator for a translation, thus acting as the initiator of the translation process. In an ideal case, the client would give as many details as possible about the purpose, explaining the addressees, time, place, occasion and medium of the intended communication and the function the text is intended to have. This information would constitute an explicit translation brief (Nord, 2001: 60):

1) the (intended) text function(s);
2) the TT receiver(s);
3) the (prospective) time and place of text reception;
4) the medium over which the text will be transmitted;
5) the motive for the production or reception of the text.

However, the Skopos often has to be negotiated between the client and the translator, especially when the client has only a vague or even incorrect idea of what kind of text is needed for the situation in question. Clients do not normally bother to give the translator an explicit translation brief (Nord, 2001: 30). If the translation brief does not tell the translator how to conduct the translation, what translation strategy to use, or what translation type to choose, then it is the translator's responsibility and competence to figure out what information in ST should be included in the TT with the most appropriate translation strategies. In many cases, an experienced translator can work out the translation Skopos by himself and adequately achieves the intended purpose of the target text.

The Skopos rule can be used to tackle a series of dilemmatic issues, such as literal translation vs. free translation, dynamic equivalence vs. formal equivalence, flexible translation vs. conservative translation, etc. All these will be decided by the Skopos of a translation which, in turn, directs the translation strategies. For example, in many cases, a relatively literal translation is exactly what is required by the receiver (commissioner or client), for instance, the translation of a marriage certificate, driver's license, foreign legal documentation and quotation in news reports, while for some other practical writings such as operational manual and advertisements, the translator may resort to such strategies as substitution, paraphrasing, adaptation, etc. in order to enhance the comprehensibility and acceptability of the version.

In terms of Skopostheorie, the viability of the brief depends on the circumstances of the target culture, not on the source culture. This leads to another more specific aspect of Skopostheorie, namely the relationship between the source and target texts within a functionalist framework.

1.3.2 Coherence rule

The coherence rule, also known as "intratexual coherence", specifies that a translation should be acceptable in a sense that it is coherent with the receivers' situation (Reiss & Vermeer, 1984: 113). Being "coherent with" is synonymous with being "part of" the receiver's situation, which indicates that a translation should be understandable and meaningful to the target readers in the target culture.

Vermeer (1989) claims that any source text is just an offer of information, and a receiver selects from it what he thinks important or interesting. It is obvious that the translator has to select and process certain items from the source text in order to form a new offer of information in the target language. What items will be chosen and translated depends on the Skopos rule, and the selection should be able to give a meaningful rendition in the target culture, i.e., it should abide by the intratextual coherence rule.

The coherence rule stipulates that, given the users' background knowledge and their situational circumstances, the target text must be sufficiently coherent to allow the intended users to understand it and interpret it under specific situation.

1.3.3 Fidelity rule

Since a translation is an offer of information from the source text, it is expected to bear some kind of relationship with the corresponding source text. Vermeer calls this relationship "intertexual coherence" or "fidelity". This is postulated as a further principle, referred to as the "fidelity rule" (Reiss & Vermeer, 1984: 114). Intertextual coherence lies between the source text and the target text, while formally, it depends on how the translator interprets the source text and the translation Skopos.

Intertextual coherence is considered subordinate to intratextual coherence, and both are subordinate to the Skopos rule. If the Skopos demands a change of function, then the required standard will no longer be intertextual coherence between ST and TT but adequacy or appropriateness with regard to the Skopos (Reiss & Vermeer, 1984: 139).

In the framework of Skopostheorie, the focus is shifted from the source text to the target text and its communicative function or functions. It is no longer the ST which sets the standards for the translator's decisions in the translation process, but the intended receiver of the translation, whose reception will be entirely guided by target reader's expectations, conventions, norms, models, real-world knowledge, perspective, etc.

This is a pragmatic model in that it takes target-orientation seriously and even makes the target receiver the most important determinant of translational decisions. It is culture-oriented because it considers translation as a "cross-cultural event" (Snell-Hornby, 1987: 82).

1.4　Manttari's Translational Action Theory

As a Finland-based German translation scholar, Justa Holz-Manttari presents the theory of translational action in her book *Translational Action: Theory and Method* in 1984, which views translation as purpose-driven, outcome-oriented human interaction to cover all forms of intercultural transfer. In this model, translation is defined as "a complex action designed to achieve a particular purpose" (Nord, 2001: 13). Like Vermeer, she holds that translation is a form of action across culture instead of a transcoding process. She uses translation behavior to replace translation because she believes that translation is a kind of transformation behavior centered on the source language text, while translation behavior is a more complex activity, aiming to achieve the cross-cultural and cross-linguistic transformation of information.

A translational action is actually an interpersonal interaction between agents who are people involved in the process of translation. These agents play certain roles in the translation process and are interconnected through a complex network of mutual relations. The agents include,

1) The initiator: the company or individual starts off the translation process and determines the purpose of the target text.

2) The commissioner: the individual who asks the translator to produce a target text for a specified purpose.

3) The ST producer: the individual who produces the source text for a translation action.

4) The TT producer, who is the translator.

5) The TT receiver, who is the final recipient of the TT.

The above participants in the translation process are not absolute, because one participant can play several roles at one time. For example, a translator who translates a book and sends it to a publishing house for printing acts as the initiator as well as the translator.

In this model, the ST is dethroned and the translation is judged not by equivalence of meaning but by its adequacy to the functional goal of the TT situation as defined by the commission.

This is quite different from the traditional concept simply involving three agents of ST author, translator and TT reader, which complements functionalist theory and widens its application to a broader scope of communication (Nord, 2001:12-13). She also paid more attention to the translator's subjectivity. However, the translation action theory also had its limitations. First, the terminology she used was more complex; secondly, the status of the original text is marginalized.

1.5 Nord's Function Plus Loyalty Theory

1.5.1 Function plus loyalty

Skopos theory, in spite of its advantages in translation, has limitations. According to Skopos theory, all the translation procedures are decided by the translation purpose. This seems acceptable when the translation purpose is in line with the communicative intentions of the original author. But a translation purpose may be contrary to or incompatible with the intention of the original writer. If the translator adapts or changes the text just for the sake of translation purpose, probably he will be criticized by the original writer for misrepresentation or falsification of the original. Functionalism is criticized for disrespecting the original, as Nord (2001:119) has admitted that "functionalist approaches are often criticized for changing or betraying originals..."

To solve problems of radical functionalism, Christiane Nord added the concept of "loyalty" to the conventional functionalism. In the 1990s, Nord first proposed the concept of function plus loyalty in her book *Text Analysis in Translation*, which further expanded the functional teleology. She (2001:126) stated:

My personal version of the functionalist approach thus stands on two pillars: function plus loyalty. Function refers to the factors that make a target text work in the intended way in the target situation. Loyalty refers to the interpersonal relationship between the translator, the source-text sender, the target-text receivers and the initiator.

Loyalty is different from faithfulness or fidelity. The latter two concepts usually refer to the relationship between source text and target text, while loyalty refers to a social relationship between people. By Loyalty, Nord refers to a kind of responsibility, a commitment to not only target text but source text and original writer as well. In fact, the notion of loyalty has added to the translator another task besides translating, that's the responsibility for mediation. In other words, the translator should consider interests of initiators (or commissioners), TT receivers and original authors, and to be a coordinator in case of conflict between the above three partners of the translation.

1.5.2 Text functions

Based on the model elaborated by the German psychologist Karl Buhler and the Czech functionalist Roman Jakobson, Christiane Nord establishes four basic textual functions (as Table 2 shows): referential function, expressive function, appellative function and phatic function.

Table 2 A Translation-Oriented Model of Textual Functions (Adapted from Nord, 2003:4)

Basic Textual Functions	Functions	Examples
referential function (*reference to objects and phenomena of the world*)	1) informative function	e. g. a traffic accident
	2) metalinguistic function	e. g. a particular use of language
	3) instructive function	e. g. the correct way of handling a washing-machine
	4) teaching function	e. g. Geography
expressive function (*expression of the sender's attitude or feelings towards the objects and phenomena*)	1) emotive function	expression of feelings, e. g. in interjections
	2) evaluative function	expression of evaluation, e. g. in a political commentary
appellative function (*i. e. appealing to the receiver's experience, feelings, knowledge, sensibility, etc. in order to induce him/her to react in a specific way*)	1) illustrative function	intended reaction: recognition of something known
	2) persuasive function	intended reaction: adopt the sender's viewpoint
	3) imperative function	intended reaction: do what the sender is asking for
	4) pedagogical function	intended reaction: learn certain forms of behavior
	5) advertising function	intended reaction: buy the product
phatic function (*i. e. establishing, maintaining or finishing contact*)	1) salutational function	
	2) "small-talk" function	
	3) "peg" function	e. g. text introductions, such as the allusion to a proverb

1.5.3 Documentary translation and instrumental translation

As for different types of text, Nord (2001) proposed two types of translation (as Table 3 and Table 4 show). One is documentary translation and the other is instrumental translation. A "documentary translation" is a kind of metatext marked as a translation (e. g. by stating the source and/or the name of the translator), whereas "instrumental translations" are object texts which can serve any function a non-translated text can achieve.

Table 3 Documentary Translation (Adapted from Nord, 2001:48)

Type of Translation	Documentary Translation			
function of translation	Document of source-culture communicative interaction for target-culture readers			
function of target text	Metatextural function			
form of translation	interlineal literal	literal transaltion	philological translation	exoticizing translation

continued

Type of Translation	Documentary Translation			
purpose of translation	reproduction of SL system	reproduction of SL form	reproduction of SL form + content	reproduction of SL form + content + situation
focus of translation process	structure of SL lexis + syntax	lexical units of source text	syntactical units of source text	textual units of source text
example	comparative linguistics	quotations in news text	Greek and Latin classics	modern literary prose

Table 4 Instrumental Translations (Adapted from Nord, 2001:51)

Type of Translation	Instrumental Translation		
function of translation	instrument for target-culture communicative interaction modelled according to source-culture communicative interaction		
function of target text	referential/expressive/appellative/phatic function and or subfunctions		
form of translation	equifunctional translation	heterofunctional translation	homologous translation
purpose of translation	achieve ST functions for target audience	achieve similar functions as ST	achieve homologous effect to ST
focus of translation process	functional units of ST	transferable functions of ST	degrees of ST originality
example	instructions for use	"Culliver's travels" for children	poetry translated by poet

1.5.4 Translation process

In functional translation, translation should therefore be done with a top-down procedure as shown in Figure 1.

Analysis of the above model:

Step 1 Deciding on the (intended, assigned) function of the translation (1a: documentary vs. instrumental); which functional elements of the ST will be kept and which should be adapted to the addressee's background knowledge, expectations, communicative needs, medium-restrictions, deixis requirements, etc. (1b: source text analysis)

Step 2 Deciding whether the translated text should conform to source-culture or target-culture conventions, both considering translational conventions and style.

Step 3 Considering the language differences.

Step 4 Considering the contextual aspects.

Step 5 Making the final decision with due respect to the function of the translation.

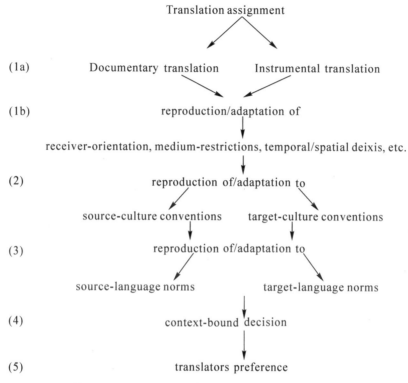

Figure 1 Procedure of a translation assignment

1.6 Newmark's Text Typology Theory

1.6.1 Text types and translation methods

Peter Newmark, a famous British translation theorist, puts forward his own text type theory. Strictly speaking, this theory does not belong to functionalist translation theory. However, it shares much common features as Reiss's text typology theory and makes a further expansion on this aspect. Therefore, it is introduced here to give insight to translation practice.

According to Peter Newmark, texts fall into three major types, namely the expressive, the informative and the vocative type. He also points out that the main functions of language are expressive (the subjective or "I" form), the descriptive or informative (the "it" form) and the vocative or directive or persuasive (the "you" form), the minor functions being the phatic, the metalingual and the aesthetic (Newmark, 2001: 21), and different types of text can be translated in special ways, which is shown in Table 5.

Table 5　Text Types and Translation (Newmark, 2001:40)

Text Type	Expressive	Informative	Vocative
typical examples	literature	scientific and technical reports and text books	publicity, propaganda, notice, laws
ideal style	individual	neutral, objective	persuasive or imperative
emphasis	source language	target language	target language
focus	writer (1st person)	situation (3rd person)	reader (2nd person)
method	literal	equivalent effect	equivalent effect
translation unit maximum minimum	small collocation word	medium sentence collocation	large text paragraph
language type	figurative	factual	compiling
meaning loss	considerable	small	dependent
new words and meanings	mandatory if in SL text	not permitted unless reasons given	yes, except in formal text
rare metaphors	reproduce	give sense	recreate
length	Appx. the same	slightly longer	no norm

As presented in the above table, typical expressive text includes formal works of literature (poem, novel, drama, autobiography, prose and personal letters). Informative text includes kinds of rules and regulations, laws and academic works which stresses "truth" and the fact outside the language. Its form can be textbook, technical report, newspaper, journals and thesis, etc. Vocative text treats readers as the center and its purpose is to call for readers to think and feel as the writer's aim. Notice, propagandas and advertisements all belong to this category.

According to Newmark, the central factor of an expressive text is the author's writing style, so Newmark suggests adopting the approach of semantic translation in such text translation. In other words, more emphasis should be put on source language (SL) than on target language (TL) to fully display the author's style which can be realized by comparing the syntactic and semantic differences between SL and TL. Besides, artistic value and cultural elements embedded in the texts also deserve translator's special attention.

The typical informative texts are concerned with any topic of knowledge, so the information conveyed rather than the language form is the core of this type of text. Meanwhile, the author's status in the text is anonymous. Therefore, Newmark suggests adopting the approach of communicative translation (CT) method and more efforts on TL rather than on SL should be given because the quality of TL texts is a high-stake factor influencing the effectiveness of readers' information reception and response.

The core of vocative text is the readership, the addressee. Newmark (2001: 41) uses the term "vocative" in the sense of "calling upon" the readers to act, think or feel, in fact to "react" in the way intended by the text. The function of this type of text has been given many other names including "conative", "instrumental", "operative" and "pragmatic". Recently, vocative texts are more often addressed to a readership than a reader, so the status of their authors is not important. What is important is the effect of information transmission and the readers' response. Therefore, Newmark suggests that vocative texts can be rendered by communicative translation approach because this method is aimed at smooth communication between SL authors and TL readers and prompting readers' reaction to TL texts. What's more, translators with the readers' reading habit, background in mind have much more "freedom" in dealing with the original syntax to retain the "vocativeness" of SL texts. They can rearrange the sentence structures of the text, and make the translated text natural, fluent, and easily understood.

Hence, the translator must firstly identify and analyze the text types before starting to translate an article, a book or a letter, because the type of text plays a primary role in the selection of translation strategies and methods. For example, cultural components are transferred intact in expressive text, explained with cultural terms in case of informative text and replaced by culturally equivalent terms in the vocative text.

However, few texts are purely expressive, informative or vocative. Most include all three functions, with an emphasis on one of the three in the aspects of author status, text emphasis, and language manner (Newmark, 2001: 42). Therefore, translators can make the most of these features to work out proper translation methods.

1.6.2 Semantic translation and communicative translation

The concept of semantic translation and communicative translation was first proposed by Peter Newmark in his book *Approaches to Translation* (1981).

Communicative translation attempts to produce on its readers an effect as close as possible to that obtained on the readers of the original. Semantic translation attempts to render, as closely as the semantic and syntactic structures of the second language allow, the exact contextual meaning of the original (Newmark, 1981: 38). The differences between semantic translation and communicative translation were further illustrated in Table 6 (Newmark, 1981: 65).

Table 6 Differences Between Semantic Translation and Communicative Translation

Parameter	Semantic Translation	Communicative Translation
transmitter/addressee focus	focus on the thought processes of the transmitter as an individual	subjective, TT reader focused
culture	should only help TT reader with connotations if they are a crucial part of message, remains within the SL culture	oriented towards a specific language and culture; transfers foreign elements into the TT culture
time and origin	not fixed in any time or local space; translation needs to be done anew with every generation	ephemeral and rooted in its own contemporary context
relation to ST	always "inferior" to ST; "loss" of meaning	may be "better" than the ST; "gain" of force and clarity even if loss of semantic content
use of form of SL	respect for the form of the SL, "loyalty" to ST author	if ST language forms deviate, then this must be replicated in TT, but overriding "loyalty" to TL norms
form of TL	more complex, awkward, detailed, concentrated; tendency to overtranslate	smoother, simpler, clearer, more direct, more conventional; tendency to undertranslate
text type	serious literature, autobiography, "personal effusion", any important political (or other) statement	the vast majority of texts, e.g. non-literary writing, technical and informative texts, publicity, etc.
criterion for evaluation	accuracy of reproduction of the ST	accuracy of communication of ST, message in TT

From what is discussed above, the discrepancy of semantic translation and communicative translation lies in the following aspects:

1) Semantic translation is source language biased, while communicative translation is target language biased.

2) Semantic translation is meaning and syntax oriented; but communicative translation is effect oriented.

3) Semantic translation emphasizes more on personal, individual style, whereas communicative translation emphasizes more on social effect and function of the target text.

4) Literal method is the first choice of semantic translation, but free method is the first choice of communicative translation.

5) A semantic translation tends to be more detailed, more complex, more awkward, but a communicative translation tends to be smoother, simpler, clearer, more natural, more direct, more conventional, conforming to a register, thus more accessible to readers.

6) In semantic translation, length of the sentences, positions and integrity of clauses, etc. are preserved whenever possible, while in communicative translation, formal features or original sentences are sacrificed more readily.

7) Semantic translation tends to be over-translated. It is more concentrated and detailed than the original, but communicative translation tends to be under-translated by using of "hold-all" terms.

8) Semantic translation is always inferior to the original because of loss of meaning, but communicative translation maybe better than the original because of gain in force and clarity, despite loss in semantic content.

9) Inaccuracy is always wrong in semantic translation, while a certain embroidering is allowed by communicative translation.

10) The translator has no right to improve or correct the original in semantic translation; however, the translator has the right to improve the logic and the style of the original.

11) The aim of a semantic translation is to produce a true version, i.e. an exact statement, but the target of a communicative translation is to create a "happy version", i.e. a successful act (Newmark, 2001a: 39).

However, just as Newmark (2001a: 39) pointed out that "all translation must be in some degree communicative and semantic, social and individual", there is no absolute communicative or semantic method of translation. They are in fact widely overlapping bands of methods. A translation can be more, or less semantic, communicative. Even a section or sentence can be treated more communicatively or less semantically.

1.7 Significance of Functionalist Translation Theory

To sum up, reader-oriented and target-culture-emphasized, Skopostheorie considers translation as a form of human interaction which is determined by its purpose or skopos. One of the most important factors is the intended receiver or addressee with specific communicative needs. Thus, the focus is shifted from the source text to the target text and its communicative function or functions. The source text is no longer the first and foremost criterion for the translator's decisions. Instead, it functions just as one of the various sources of information which can be adjusted or even adapted according to the intended function of the target text and target-text receiver's culture, expectations, conventions, real world knowledge, etc.

As a result, a translator generally acts as a receiver of both the commissioner's instructions and the source text. After agreeing with the commissioner on the conditions involved, he/she is supposed to be able to justify a particular purpose in a given translation situation, select from the source text the most crucial and important information for target readers and present them in a manner that helps to fulfill the intended function of the target text.

Functional model is pragmatic in that it is cultural-oriented because it considers transition as a cross-cultural event (Snell-Hornby, 1987: 82). It is a model which gives due consideration to the role of the translator as an expert set free from submissive "servants" who do what they are told by the source text, but fully responsible partners in a cooperative interaction between equals—no less, no more (Trosborg, 2012: 25).

It shifts translation from a "bottom-up" process, which works from the linguistic text-surface structures up and finally pragmatics, to a top-down stages which starts from pragmatics to conventions and finally to linguistic text-surface structures. This can guarantee the realization of communicative need, for it draws focus from linguistic elements to pragmatic functions.

In a sense, Skopostheorie is particularly operative and applicable in translating practical texts. Functionalist approach opens up a new perspective for both translation theory studies and practice. One might thus suppose that once "discovered" (not as something unheard of before, but as something that had always been there without anyone really noticing) it would spread like wildfire through the world of translation studies (Nord, 2001:129).

Chapter Two   Contrastive Study Between English and Chinese

Each language has its own habitual way of expression, and the differences between languages give rise to problems in the translation process. Eugene A. Nida (1984: 25) proposed that the action of translation is "decoding the meaning of a text in one language and encoding it into a different language"..., so no matter what principles to follow, what cultural factors to consider and what functions to achieve in translation, the transformation of the original language to the target language is an inevitable step. As for the Chinese to English translation or vice versa, a comparative study of the language features can provide valuable support for the solution of the code-switching problems.

2.1 Differences in Word Order

Word order, as defined by *Dictionary of Language and Linguistics*, is "the placing of words in a sequence according to the conventions of a given language" (Hartmann & Stork, 1972). It refers to the sequence or relative position of words not only in a sentence (Pei, 1954), but also in a clause or a phrase (Pei & Gaynor, 1966). More recently in *Oxford Concise Dictionary of Linguistics*, "word order" is used to describe the order of phrases as well as words (Matthews, 2007). It refers to order of elements such as subject, verb, object, predicative and adverbial in the context of clauses or sentences, not just the order of individual words. In other words, word order can be understood as order of syntactic structures.

As English and Chinese belongs to different language families, the word order is different in many ways.

2.1.1 Difference in basic word order in the simple sentence

Basic word order of English sentence: subject + predicate + object + manner adverbial + place adverbial + time adverbial

Basic word order of Chinese sentence: subject + time adverbial + place adverbial + manner adverbial + predicate + object

For example:

(1) ①They ②discussed ③the plan ④animatedly ⑤in the classroom ⑥yesterday

afternoon.

①他们 ⑥昨天下午 ⑤在教室里 ④热烈地 ②讨论 ③这个计划。

(2)①The new students ②were working ③at the physics laboratory ④from 8 to 12 this morning.

①新同学 ④今天上午八点到十二点 ③在物理实验室 ②做实验。

(3)①I think to ②succeed ③in different markets ④you really have to ⑤look at the consumers ⑥from their perspective ⑦and really try to understand Chinese consumers' behavior in the market.

①我相信要 ③在不同市场 ②获得成功 ④就必须 ⑥从消费者的角度 ⑤来看待问题 ⑦要切实理解中国消费者的市场行为。

2.1.2 Differences in attributes and translation methods

Both English and Chinese have attributes to modify noun, noun phrases and pronouns. However, the position of attributes in English and Chinese is quite different. In English, short attribute (single word) is usually placed in front of the words it modifies. If the attribute is relatively long, i.e. a prepositional/infinitive/participle phrase or a clause, it is often put after the antecedent. While in Chinese, an attribute, no matter short or long, is always placed in front of the antecedent. For example(ST stands for source text; TT stands for target text):

(1) ST: The <u>intrinsic</u> quality of a work of art is starting to seem like its least <u>important</u> property.

TT:一件艺术品的内在品质似乎开始成为它最不重要的属性。

(2) ST: Prior to the twentieth century, women in novels were also subject to numerous restrictions <u>imposed by the male-dominated culture.</u>

TT:在20世纪以前,小说中的妇女要屈从于<u>由男性主宰的文化传统强加给</u>她们的种种束缚。

(3) ST: They were forced to put forward an alternative <u>of separate development for all races in this so-called homelands</u>, with a promise of eventual independence for the Africans in these areas.

TT:他们不得不变换花样,提出所有种族在自己的所谓本土上分别发展的办法,并许诺非洲人最终在这些地区获得独立。

(4) ST: Do you want to see the doctor <u>working on the case report in the office?</u>

TT:你要见那位<u>正在办公室里写病历的</u>医生吗?

(5) ST: The second aspect is the application by all the members in a society, from the government official to the ordinary citizen, of the special methods of thought and action <u>that scientists use in their work.</u>

TT:第二方面是使用<u>科学家们在工作中所运用的</u>特殊的思想方法和行动方法。社会所有成员,从政府官员到普通百姓,都要使用这些方法。

(6) ST: For the millions <u>who lack access to good, in-person education</u>, online learning

Chapter Two   Contrastive Study Between English and Chinese

can open doors that would otherwise remain closed.

　　TT：对于那些无法获得良好的个人教育的人来说，在线学习可以为其敞开紧闭的大门。

　　（7）ST：As a result, they often focused on those sections of MOOCs that provided the specific knowledge they sought, and neglected the other sections.

　　TT：因此，他们往往把重点放在那些提供他们所寻求的具体知识的 MOOC 部分，而忽略了其他部分。

　　Therefore, in E-C translation, many long attributes including attributive clauses are translated before the antecedent it modifies as in example （2） to （7）. However, the attributive clauses are not always translated before the antecedent it modifies. There are mainly two reasons. The first reason is that very long attributes before the antecedent sometimes makes the Chinese sentence difficult to understand or sound awkward. The second reason is that some attributive sentences in English have the function of reason, result, purpose or condition. In such cases, English attributive sentences can be translated separately. We can compare version 1 with version 2 in the following examples to see the point.

　　（1）ST：I put on my clothes by the light of moon just setting, where rays streamed through the narrow window near my crib.

　　TT1：趁着床边窄窄的窗户透过来的正在西沉的月光，我穿上了衣服。

　　TT2：一轮明月渐渐西坠，月光透过小床边一个窄窄的窗子射了进来，我趁着月光穿上了衣服。

　　（2）ST：China and Japan reached agreement on the issue of agriculture which was a major barrier for their bilateral relation since 1996.

　　TT1：中日两国最终就自一九九六年起就是两国关系发展的主要障碍的农业问题达成了协议。

　　TT2：中日两国最终就农业问题达成了协议，而该问题自一九九六年起就是两国关系发展的主要障碍。

　　Analysis：In the above two example, the first versions read a little awkward, while the second ones are much more in line with Chinese expression habit and more forceful in effect. The translation method used in TT2 is translating the attributive sentence into an independent one through repeating the antecedent.

　　（3）ST：Behaviorists suggest that the child who is raised in an environment where there are many stimuli which develop his or her capacity for appropriate responses will experience greater intellectual development.

　　TT1：行为主义认为生长在有很多能够发展孩子做出适当反应的能力的刺激环境下的孩子将会有更好的智力发展。

　　TT2：行为主义认为如果一个儿童在有很多刺激物的环境里成长，而这些刺激物又能够发展其做出适当反应的能力，那么，这个儿童将会有更好的智力发展。

　　Analysis：There are three attributive sentences in this example. If they are put before the antecedents being modified as in TT1, the meaning becomes confused and it sounds unnatural to Chinese, so they translated flexibly in TT2 which is more smooth and readable.

The following are more examples showing the flexible methods of E-C translation of attributive clauses.

(4) ST: Day and night are very long on the moon, where one day is as long as two weeks.

TT: 在月亮上,白天和黑夜都相当长,月亮上的一天等于地球上的两周。

(5) ST: We wish to express our satisfaction at this to the Special Committee, whose activities deserve to be encouraged.

TT: 我们对特别委员会表示满意,特别委员会的工作值得受到鼓励。

(6) ST: One was a violent thunderstorm, the worst I had ever seen, which obscured my objective.

TT: 有一次暴风骤雨,猛烈的程度实在是我平生所鲜见的。这场暴风雨遮住了我的目标。

Analysis: Most unrestricted attributive clauses as example (4), (5) and (6) are translated as independent clauses by repeating the antecedents.

(7) ST: After dinner, the four key negotiators resumed their talks which continued well into the night.

TT: 饭后,四个主要谈判人继续进行会谈,一直谈到深夜。

(8) ST: This was the period when Newton began the research which resulted in the creation of his famous Theory of Gravity.

TT: 就在这期间,牛顿开始了这项研究。经过这项研究,他创立了著名的引力理论。

Analysis: Some attributive clauses are translated into independent clauses following the headwords by omitting the antecedents as in example (7) and (8).

(9) ST: The manager was giving a dinner for a few people whom he wished especially to talk to or to hear from.

TT: 经理只宴请了几个人,因为他特别想和这些人谈谈,听听他们的意见。(translated into causative adverbial clause)

(10) ST: This company, which wants to get their new product sold well in the market, is trying hard to perfect its packing and workmanship.

TT: 为了使新产品在市场热销,这个公司正在全力改进工艺和外包装。(translated into adverbial clause of purpose)

(11) ST: A new product which has beautiful packing, good quality and advertising may very likely be a hit in market.

TT: 一种新产品,只要包装精美、质量过硬、宣传得力,就能在市场中热销。(translated into adverbial of condition)

(12) ST: The two countries established formal diplomatic relation, which paved the way for the further communication.

TT: 两国正式建立了外交关系,从而为双方进一步的交流铺平了道路。(translated into adverbial of result)

Chapter Two Contrastive Study Between English and Chinese

(13) ST: My assistant, who had carefully read through the instructions before doing his experiment, could not obtain satisfactory results, because he followed them too mechanically.

TT:虽然我的助手在做实验前已从头到尾仔细阅读过说明,但由于他生搬硬套,所以没能得到满意的结果。(translated into adverbial of concession)

(14) ST: Thousands of overseas have asked to be permitted to return to China, but they have met with all sorts of unreasonable obstacles, which have prevented them from returning to their motherland.

TT:成千上万的中国侨民要求回国,但受到种种无理阻挠,以致无法回到祖国。(translated into adverbial of result)

Analysis: If an attributive clause states the reason, concession or result, it can be translated as adverbial as in example (9), (10), (11), (12), (13) and (14).

2.1.3 Differences in adverbial and translation methods

In Chinese, adverbial of time, cause, condition or concession always precedes the main clause, while in English, the word order is flexible depending mainly on coherence. For example:

如果明天不下雨,运动会将照常举行。

The sports meeting will be held as scheduled if it doesn't rain tomorrow.

OR:

If it doesn't rain tomorrow, the sports meeting will be held as scheduled.

Therefore, in E-C translation, if the adverbial clause follows the main clause in English, it should be placed before the main clause in Chinese. For example:

(1) ST: Modern scientific and technical books, especially textbooks, requires revision at short intervals if their authors wish to keep pace with new ideas, observations and discoveries.

TT:对于现代科技图书,特别是教科书来说,要是作者希望自己书中的内容能与新概念、新观察到的事实和新发现同步发展的话,那么就应该每隔较短的时间,将书中的内容重新修订。

(2) ST: He was given a chair and asked to wait a little as darkness came on, then suddenly the whole bridge was outlined in lights.

TT:天快黑了,有人给了他一把椅子,请他坐下等一会儿。忽然电灯全亮了,照出了整座大桥的轮廓。

(3) ST: My family and I were surprised and joyful after hearing the news that I got a position in Microsoft.

TT:得知我在微软公司谋得一份工作这一消息之后,我和家人既吃惊又高兴。

(4) ST: People were afraid to leave their houses, for although the police had been ordered to stand by in case of emergency, they were just as confused and helpless as anybody else.

TT：尽管警察已接到命令，要做好准备以应付紧急情况，但人们还是不敢出门，因为警察也和其他人一样不知所措和无能为力。

（5）ST：Nowadays it is understood that a diet which contains nothing harmful may result in serious disease if certain important elements are missing.

TT：如今人们知道，如果食物中缺少了某些重要的成分，即使其中不含有任何有害的物质，也会引起严重的疾病。

2.1.4　Differences in logic sequence and translation methods

Different perception and thinking modes between English and Chinese lead to the discrepancy in sentence construction. Generally speaking, Chinese often organize the sentence in an inductive way, i. e. from background to foreground, from general to specific, from the event that happens first to the event that happens later. However, English prefers a deductive way of organizing ideas, which is not often in accordance with the Chinese one. Therefore, it is necessary for translators to reconstruct (adjust) or even reverse the order of the source text to achieve better effect in translation. This is especially true when it comes to translating long sentences. For example：

（1）ST：It would have been difficult to find a happier child than I was as I lay in my crib at the close of that eventful day and lived over the joys it had brought me, and for the first time longed for a new day to come.

TT：在这个意义重大的日子即将结束的时候，我躺在自己的小床上回顾一天的快乐，第一次渴望着新的一天的到来。恐怕再也找不到比我更幸福的小孩子了。

（2）ST：Such is human nature in the West that a great many people are often willing to sacrifice higher pay for the privilege of becoming white collar workers.

TT：许多人常常宁愿牺牲高薪以换取成为白领工人的社会地位。这在西方倒是人之常情。

（3）ST：He was puzzled that I did not want what was obviously a "step" toward what all Americans are taught to want when they grow up：money and power.

TT：一般来说，金钱和权力是所有美国人长大后都想要追求的东西，而我并不想要，对此他疑惑不解。

（4）ST：No one will deny that what we have been able to do in the past five years is especially striking in view of the crisis which we inherited from the previous government.

TT：考虑到上届政府遗留下来的危机，我们在过去5年里所取得的成绩尤为显著。这是不可否认的。

（5）ST：For a family of four, for example, it is more convenient as well as cheaper to sit comfortably at home, watching TV, with almost unlimited entertainment available, than to go out in search of amusement elsewhere.

TT：譬如，对于一个四口之家来说，舒舒服服地在家中看电视，就能看到几乎数不清的娱乐节目。这比到别的地方去消遣更便宜更方便。

（6）ST：In a word, it is in line with the interests for both sides to seek common

Chapter Two Contrastive Study Between English and Chinese

development and to deal with their differences with pragmatic attitude.

TT：总之，寻求共同发展并以务实的态度对待双方的分歧是符合双方的共同利益的。

(7) ST：This preface must necessarily be short and modest, for I cannot claim to be an expert in painting, merely an ardent lover of the art.

TT：我在绘画方面谈不上有所专攻，只是热爱这门艺术而已，因此要为这部画册作序，只能三言两语谈一点肤浅的看法。

(8) ST：Aluminum remained unknown until the nineteenth century, because nowhere in nature is it found free, owing to its always being combined with other elements, most commonly with oxygen, for which it has a strong affinity.

TT：铝总是跟其他元素结合在一起，最普遍的是跟氧结合；因为铝具有强烈的亲氧性，在自然界找不到游离状态的铝。因此，铝直到19世纪才被人发现。

(9) ST：He flew yesterday from Beijing where he spent his vacation after finishing the meeting he had taken part in Tianjin.

TT：他本来在天津开会，会议一结束，他就去北京度假了，昨天才坐飞机回来。

2.2 Hypotaxis of English vs. Parataxis of Chinese

Eugene Nida (1982: 16) points out, "For Chinese and English, perhaps one of the most important linguistic distinctions is the contrast between the hypotaxis and parataxis. English pays more attention to the integrity of sentence structures. No matter how long and complicated an English sentence is, its form remains compact rather than diffusive. There are mainly two reasons for this.

The first reason is that many compact devices are employed in English sentences, such as the frequent use of prepositions like *of*, *with*, *from*, *in*, *on*, *by*, *to*, and prepositional phrases like *with the help of*, *at the speed of*, *with a ratio of*, *under the guidance of*, and the use of various connectives, which clearly indicate the relation between different sentence elements. For example, relative pronoun (*who*, *which*, *whom*, *that*, *whose*), relative adverb (*when*, *why*, *where*, *how*), conjunctions (*and*, *or*, *therefore*, *because*, *so*, *as a result*, *as soon as*, *once*, *if*, *although*, *but*) are often employed in long sentences to link and indicate the relation of the main clause and the subordinate.

The second reason is that English is a kind of inflected language. Inflection, variations or changes that words undergo such as gerund, present participle, past participle, and word derivation indicate their relations with other words and changes in meaning. All these result in the preponderance of compound-complex sentences in English.

Although there are some connectives in Chinese, Chinese people show a natural tendency of using less or no connectives. The relations of the constituents in a Chinese sentence or those between the sentences are displayed indirectly through the logic order. O. Jesperson (1954: 57) once commented: "Chinese of the old style carries with it an impressive dignity through the immediate succession of nothing but momentous notions; it requires a simple greatness because it throws away all unnecessary accessory elements and thus, as it were, takes flight to pure thinking." The famous Chinese linguist Liu Xie also pointed out that a Chinese sentence is built on the basis of amalgamation of characters and the amalgamation of characters makes a sentence; the accumulation of sentences makes a text (Lian Shuneng, 1993: 65), so Chinese sentences tend to be diffusive with loose structures mixed by both complete sentences and a series of phrases.

Therefore, in E-C translation, hypotactic English sentences are often translated into Chinese paratactic sentences by omitting connectives or prepositions. And the long compact sentences have to be divided and restructured into Chinese diffusive sentences. For example:

(1) ST: A body in motion remains in motion <u>at</u> a constant speed <u>in</u> a straight line <u>unless</u> acted upon by an external force

TT: 没有外力作用,运动的物体就连续做匀速直线运动。

(2) ST: Trying to pass another car <u>while</u> traveling at high speed brought serious injury to two men last night <u>when</u> their automobile overturned twice on Washington Boulevard at Potter Avenue.

TT: 昨晚,波特大街的华盛顿大道口发生车祸,两名驾车男子严重受伤,车子试图在高速超越另一辆车时连打了两个滚。

(3) ST: The fans are often fitted with movable shutters to their air intakes <u>which</u> open and close automatically <u>under the control of</u> thermostats to the cylinder temperatures as even as possible, admitting more air <u>when</u> the engine is working hard and less <u>when</u> it is idling.

TT: 通风机的进气口通常安装有带活动叶片的百叶窗,叶片在恒温器的控制下可以自动开关,以保证汽缸的温度尽可能恒定,发动机紧张工作时让更多的空气进入,而发动机空转时尽量减少空气进入。

(4) ST: Today the high-tech marketplace is an intensely competitive area, and a number of entrepreneurs who left the shelter of major corporations or academia to set out on their own have discovered <u>that</u> it is not enough to have a good idea, or even a good product, <u>in order to</u> start a corporation that will survive amid the giants of domestic and foreign competition.

TT: 今天的高科技市场竞争十分激烈,为数不少的企业家在脱离了大公司和院校的荫护而自谋发展之后发现,为了能够在国内外强大的竞争中生存下去,仅靠一个好的想法,甚至一个好产品是不行的。

(5) ST: It is believed by the party leaders <u>that</u> the "middle-of-the-road" candidate—the man <u>who</u> does not represent either the extremely liberal attitude or the extremely conservative attitude—is more likely to succeed than man <u>who</u> represents one extreme or the other.

TT: 这些政党领导人认为,采取中间路线的候选人既不是极端的自由主义者,也不是极端的保守主义者,竞选中推出这种人比代表这一极端或那一极端的人更可能获胜。

Obviously, all the long English sentences above are tightly connected by different grammatical devices or connectives to keep integrity, while the Chinese versions tend to be

Chapter Two Contrastive Study Between English and Chinese

diffusive without resorting to the same number of connectives.

However, when we translate Chinese sentences into English, we should carefully analyze the logical relations among the clauses and detect the implied meaning and bring it out explicitly in the English version. Specifically speaking, in most cases, we should reconstruct the original structure by combining clusters of short, loose Chinese sentences into long and compact English sentences through adding necessary connectives and prepositions. For example:

(1) ST：人不犯我,我不犯人;人若犯我,我必犯人。

TT：We will not attack <u>unless</u> we are attacked; if we are attacked, we will certainly counter attack.

(2) ST：谁会想到,在这个世纪开始之时,最伟大的贡献之一竟来自两个默默无闻、不为人知的美国青年。他们探索人类思想的极限,使我们能够第一次在空中飞行,在夕阳外翱翔。

TT：We would have thought <u>that</u> as this century opened <u>that</u> one of the greatest contributions would come from two obscure, fresh-faced young Americans <u>who</u> pursed the utmost bounds of human thought, <u>and</u> gave us all, for the first time, the power to literally sail beyond the sunset, soaring on the air.

(3) ST：灾难深重的中华民族,一百年来,其优秀人物奋斗牺牲,前赴后继,摸索救国救民的真理,是可歌可泣的。

TT：For a hundred years, the excellent sons and daughters of the disaster-ridden Chinese nation fought <u>and</u> sacrificed their lives, one stepping into the breach <u>as</u> another fell, <u>in quest of</u> truth <u>that</u> would save the country and the people. This is really chantable.

(4) ST：在经济发展中,我们要控制人口、节约资源、保护环境,并把它们放到重要位置上。

TT：Great importance must be attached to population control, the conservation of resources and environmental protection in economic growth.

(5) ST：全党通知一定要充分认识反腐败斗争的长期性、复杂性、艰巨性,把反腐倡廉建设放在更加突出的位置,旗帜鲜明地反对腐败。

TT：All party members must be fully aware <u>that</u> fighting corruption will be a protracted, complicated and arduous battle, attach great importance to combating corruption <u>and</u> upholding integrity <u>and</u> take a clear stand against corruption.

In the above examples, Chinese loose diffusive sentences are combined into English integrity sentences in translation. However, in some cases, long complicated diffusive Chinese sentences may be separated into two or more sentences in translation by semantic groups which are paralleled, transited from general to specific or verse visa. For example:

(1) ST：这一点现在就必须向党内讲明白,务必使同志们继续保持谦虚、谨慎、不骄、不燥的作风,务必使同志们继续保持艰苦奋斗的作风。

TT：This must be made clear now in the Party. The comrades must be taught to remain modest, prudent and free from arrogance and rashness in their style of work. The comrades must be taught to preserve the style of plain living and hard struggle.

(2) ST：古来一切有成就的人,都很严肃地对待自己的生命。他活着一天,总要尽量多劳动、多工作、多学习，不肯虚度年华，不让时间白白地浪费掉。

TT: Throughout the ages, all people of accomplishment take their lives seriously. As long as they are alive, they would rather devote themselves to more work and study than let a single minute slip by in vain.

（3）ST：要抓紧时机，加快发展，实施科教兴国战略、人才强国战略和可持续发展战略，充分发挥科学技术作为第一生产力的作用，依靠科技进步，提高劳动者素质，促进国民经济又好又快发展。

TT: The party must lose no time in speeding up development, implement the strategy of rejuvenating the country through science and education with trained personnel and the strategy of sustainable development, to give full play to the role of science and technology as the primary production force. The Party must take advantage of the advance of science and technology to improve the quality of workers and promote sound and rapid development of the national economy.

（4）ST：外文出版社专事外文图书的编辑出版，几十年来用外语翻译出版了大量的中国文学作品和文化典籍，上自先秦，下迄现当代，力求全面而准确地反映中国文学及中国文化的基本面貌和灿烂成就。

TT: Foreign Languages Press is dedicated to the editing, translating and publishing of books in foreign languages. Over the past several decades, it has published, in English, a great number of China's classics and records as well as literary works from the Pre-Qin Period down to modern times, in the aim to fully display the best part of the Chinese culture and achievements.

2.3 English Subject-Predicate Structure vs. Chinese Topic-Comment Structure

2.3.1 Topic predominant Chinese sentence structure

The subject-predicate structure has absolute predominance in English, but it is not the case in Chinese which is not only demonstrated by simple sentences but also by complicated sentences. Apart from subject-predicate structure sentences in Chinese, there is another type of sentence structure in which the relationship between the word in the subject position and the verb in the predicate position are not actor and actions. This kind of sentence is interpreted by the famous Chinese linguist Chao Y. R. in his *A Grammar of Spoken Chinese* (1968:45) as "topic and comment". The topic here refers to something that the speaker brings up to be talked about, namely, the theme. The rest of the sentence following the topic is the comment in which the theme is developed, commented, explained or questioned, which is also known as the rheme. The comment/rheme may be a verb, verb phrases, or a serial of short phrases or clauses, which differ greatly from the subject-predicate English sentences. This kind of sentences is very common in descriptive writing such as the description of a person, a book, a scenery spots or an object. The following are some typical examples with their English versions.

(1) ST：江南,秋当然也是有的;但草木凋得慢,空气来得润,天的颜色显得淡,并且时常多雨而少风。

TT：There is of course autumn in the South too, but the plants wither slowly, the air is moist, the sky pallid, and it is mope rainy than windy. (Translated by Zhang Peiji)

(2) ST：郁达夫的小说有鲜明的特色,描写十分大胆、率直,有细腻的心理刻画,有直抒胸臆的抒情,多用"自叙传"的方式和第一人称的写法,文笔优美,富有诗意特征。

TT：Yu Dafu's novels had distinctive features, being fearless and straightforward in portrayal, careful and detailed in description of man's psychology and outpouring of passions. In beautiful language and highly poetic, most of his works were written in the first person tone.

(3) ST：芦笙是中国苗族、侗族等少数民族在祭奉祖先或喜庆丰收时用来吹奏的一种吹管乐器,由芦笙竹管和两根吹气管装在木制的座子上制成,高者逾两丈,小者尺许。

TT：Lusheng, a reed-type wind instrument, is often played by Miao or Dong ethic people to celebrate their harvest or to worship ancestors. The length of a Lusheng ranges from about 6 meters of the longest one to about 0.3 meter of the shortest.

As is shown in the above example, Chinese topic-comment structure is often rendered into English subject-predicate structure by employing different means of cohesion to combine the phrases into a sentence or by reorganizing it into several sentences.

2.3.2 Subject-predicate structure of English language

Unlike Chinese, the core structure of the English sentence is subject-predicate no matter how long the sentence is. In E-C translation, most sentences have to be changed to cater for Chinese way of expression. For example:

(1) ST：This is an intelligently organized and fervant meeting in a packed Town Hall with Mr. Blacks in the chair.

TT：这是一次精心组织的会议,市政大厅里济济一堂,热情洋溢,主持会议的是布莱克先生。

(2) ST：Prior to the twentieth century, women in novels were stereotypes of lacking any features that made them unique individuals and were also subject to numerous restrictions imposed by the male-dominated culture.

TT：在20世纪以前,小说中的妇女像都是一个模式。她们没有任何特点,因而无法成为具有个性的人;她们还要屈从于由男性主宰的文化传统强加给她们的种种束缚。

(3) ST：Congress had made laws requiring most pressure groups to give information about how much they spend and how they spent it, the amount and sources of funds, membership, and names and salaries of their representatives.

TT：国会已制定法律,要求大部分压力集团呈报它们花费了多少钱,怎样花的,款项的总额以及基金的来源、成员人数、代表的姓名和薪酬等情况。

(4) ST：Dr. Smith resumed the activities of anti-cancer experiment begun in 1975 and

financed by the Federal government as soon as he snapped from his original disappointment at repeated failures, which had resulted in their forced suspension.

TT：史密斯医生于1975年开始着手由联邦政府资助的抗癌实验。他由于屡遭失败而感到沮丧,被迫终止了实验工作。现在他又重新振作起来,继续抗癌实验活动。

2.4 Differences in Reference

Reference can be classified as personal reference, demonstrative reference and comparative reference. Personal reference is made of personal pronouns (I, you, he, she, we, they, me, him, her, them, etc.), possessive determiners (my, our, his, her, their, etc.) and possessive pronouns (his, hers, theirs, etc.). Demonstrative reference involves the selective nominal demonstratives (this, these, that, those, its, their). Reference is one of the main ways to realize cohesion in both Chinese text and English text. However, the frequency of the occurrences of the above two types of reference in Chinese is lower than that of English. Pronouns are often omitted in Chinese, which is referred to as ellipsis or zero anaphora. In other words, Chinese often leave something unsaid that is understood or inferable from the context.

As Li and Thompson (1979) have pointed out, the strategy of using a zero anaphora is very common in Chinese and is perfectly grammatical. The following are some examples and their English versions.

(1) ST：到二〇二〇年全面建设小康社会目标实现之时,我们这个历史悠久的文明古国和发展中的社会主义大国,将成为工业化基本实现,综合国力显著增强,国内市场总体规模位居世界前列的国家,成为人民富裕程度普遍提高,生活质量明显改善、生态环境良好的国家,成为人民享有更加充分民主权利,具有更高文明素质和精神追求的国家,成为各方面制度更加完善,社会更加充满活力而又安定团结的国家,成为对外更加开放,更加具有亲和力,为人类文明作出更大贡献的国家。

TT：When the goal of building a moderately prosperous society in all respects is attained by 2020, China, a large developing socialist country with an ancient civilization, will have basically accomplished industrialization, with **its** overall strength significantly increased and **its** domestic market ranking as one of the largest in the world. **It** will be a country **whose** people are better off and enjoy markedly improved quality of life and a good environment. **Its** citizens will have more extensive democratic rights, show higher ethical standards and look forward to greater cultural achievements. China will have better institutions in all areas and **Chinese** society will have greater vitality coupled with stability and unity. The country will be still more open and friendly to the outside world and make greater contributions to human civilization.

It is clear that in the above long Chinese sentence, only one pronoun ("我们") is used, but in its English version, six pronouns are added.

(2) ST：依托陈鹤琴"家园合作"的教育思想,近年来我们幼儿园在家园共育方面进行了积极的探索:既继承传统的家园联系方式,也组织家长会、亲子活动、家教论文评比等丰富多彩的活动,促进家园互动,还利用网络联系、家庭俱乐部等形式,探索家园沟通新渠道。

TT: Our kindergarten has been exploring new ways to nurture kids guided by Chen Heqin's idea of the cooperation of kindergarten and families. We not only take traditional measures to interact with kids' families but also organize parents' meeting, family club, parents and children sports meeting and other activities. Besides, we use internet and other modern ways to strengthen communications between families and the kindergarten.

(3) ST: 设备的可靠性和可维修性是设备的两个最重要的特点,不仅会影响设备的总维修费用,也会影响到设备的维修管理。

TT: Reliability and maintainability characteristics are the two most critical features of equipment **which** influence the total cost of maintenance and also **its** management.

(4) ST: 中国古代神话传说,天地万物之祖盘古死后,头部化为东岳泰山,腹为中岳,左臂为南岳,足为西岳。从而,泰山成为五岳之首。

TT: According to the Chinese ancient mythology, when Pangu, the ancestor of the earth, died, his head turned into Mount Tai; his belly into the Central Mountain; his left arm turned into the South Mountain and his right hand, the West Mountain. Mount Tai thus become the head of all the mountains.

(5) ST:从洞窗透视大瀑布,更觉得迷蒙清爽,好像置身于仙境一般。

TT: If you view the waterfall from the window, the picture will be quite obscure, which may make you wonder you have come into the fairyland.

Obviously, in the above examples, the omitted references are added to the English versions to make the meaning clearer.

In addition, Chinese prefers noun repetition, while English prefers pronoun substitutions. Attention must be paid to this difference between the two languages. The example below is taken from "The sight of Father's Back"(《背影》) in Chinese and its English version translated by Professor Zhang Peiji.

(6) ST:那年冬天,祖母死了,父亲的差使也交卸了,正是祸不单行的日子。我从北京到徐州,打算跟着父亲奔丧回家。到徐州见着父亲,看见满院狼藉的东西,又想起祖母,不禁簌簌地流下眼泪。父亲说:"事已如此,不必难过,好在天无绝人之路!"(朱自清《背影》)

TT: In that year, my grandma died and my father lost his job. I left Beijing for Xuzhou to join him in hastening home to attend my grandma's funeral. When I met him in Xuzhou, the sight of the disordering mess in our courtyard and the thought of my grandma started tears trickling down my cheeks. He said, "Now that things have come to such a pass, it's no use crying. Fortunately, Heaven always leaves one a way out."

In the original text, the word "父亲" has appeared four times, while in the English version, the word "father" only appears once, with the other three being translated into personal pronouns "his", "he" and "him".

The following are more examples:

(7) ST:失败并不是坏事,重要的是战胜失败,从失败中站起来。

TT: Failure is not a terrible thing. What really counts is to conquer it and rise above it.

(8) ST: 共同富裕的构想是这样提出的:一部分地区有条件先发展起来,一部分地区发展慢点,先发展起来的地区带动后发展的地区,最终达到共同富裕。

TT: Our plan is as follows: where conditions permit, some areas may develop faster than others. Those that develop faster can help promote the progress of those that lag behind, until all become prosperous.

(9) ST: 今天,中国人因他们许多优秀的品质而受到世界人民的普遍钦佩。在这些品质中,尤以尊重教育、肯吃苦为人民称道。

TT: Today, the Chinese are generally admired for their many remarkable characteristics. Among them the high regard for education and willingness to work hard are some noteworthy ones.

(10) ST: 公司必须丢弃一些老旧能力,获取或建立新的能力。

TT: The company must discard some of its old capabilities, acquire and build new ones.

2.5 Nominalization of English Language and Its Translation

As defined in *Oxford Dictionary of Linguistics*, nominalization is a process by which either a noun or a syntactic unit functioning as a noun phrase derived from any other kind of unit such as a verb or an adjective. In other words, nominalization refers to the process of transforming a verb, an adjective or a clause into a noun or nominal group. Nominalization is characterized by an objective, solemn and precise style which is typical of social science works, official papers, reviews of newspaper and periodicals, legal documents, and business letters, etc. in English Language. Professor Lian Shuneng (1993), an expert of English-Chinese contrastive study, also concludes that nominalization is a typical feature of English language, because nominalized structures usually convey more sophisticated ideas or complex concepts than other linguistic forms and highlight a rigorous style of formal texts in a concise, and objective manner.

There are two ways to form nouns from verbs or adjectives. One type uses the same word as a noun without any additional morphology, which is referred to as zero-derivation. The other type requires the addition of a derivational suffix to create a noun.

2.5.1 Nominalization with zero-derivation

(1) ST: With the appearance of modern means of communication and transportation, and with the advent of faster financial flow, the world is becoming smaller.

TT: 随着现代通信和交通手段的出现,以及更快速的金融流通的来临,世界变得越来越小。

(2) ST: The pressure increase out of control was at the bottom of explosion.

TT：失去控制的气压增长是这一爆炸的根本原因。

(3) ST：The rusting of iron is only one example of corrosion, which may be described as the destructive chemical attack of a metal by media with which it comes in contact, such as moisture, air and water.

TT：可以认为,腐蚀是金属接触湿气、空气和水等介质时受到的破坏性化学侵蚀,而铁生锈只是其中一个例子。

(4) ST：Conditions of rotation and heat transfer in the earth's atmosphere are such that irregular waves of the characteristics described above will form.

TT：地球大气的自转和在其中的热输送状况结果导致具有上述特征的不规则波的形成。

(5) ST：A 5-day week has found an immediate welcome and much popularity ever since.

TT：五天工作制立即受到了人们的普遍欢迎和拥护。

2.5.2 Nominalization with derivational morphology

(1) ST：COVID-19 is an acute respiratory illness in humans caused by coronavirus, which is capable of producing severe symptoms and death, especially in the elderly and others with underlying health conditions.

TT：新型冠状病毒感染是一种由冠状病毒引起的急性呼吸道疾病,能够引起重症甚至死亡,对于老年人和基础病患者尤其如此。

(2) ST：They are designing new inertial guidance systems which would guide rockets and interplanetary spaceships by using devices which detect changes in speed and direction and make necessary adjustments automatically.

TT：他们正在设计新型惯性导航系统。这种系统利用可探测速度与方向变化并自动进行必要调节的装置,给火箭和星际宇宙飞船导航。

(3) ST：In the first place, any scientific study requires that there be no preferential weighting of one or another of the items in the series it selects for its consideration.

TT：首先,任何科学研究都要求人们对所选择考察对象不能厚此薄彼。

(4) ST：Environmental degradation and population growth, with consequent increase in demand for water, have contributed to a shortage of good quality fresh water.

TT：环境退化和人口增长,以及随之而来的对水需求的不断增加,使优质淡水的短缺变得更加严重。

(5) ST：An examination of all the variables in the test concluded that the unusually good results were due to the way he had handled the mice, the way he talked to them and the tone, the confidence, the reassurance, and the certainty in his voice.

TT：对实验中所有变量进行检查可以得出结论:这些结果非同寻常地好,是因为他对待老鼠的方式,对它们讲话的方式和语调,他声音中的信心、安抚和坚定。

By adding a suffix, a verbal adjective can be changed into a noun. The following table shows the derivation process.

Table 7　Nominalization derivation process.

Suffix	Examples
-tion	alternate—alternation, apply—application, demonstrate—demonstration, realize—realization, contribute—contribution, organize—organization, examine—examination
-sion	decide—decision, conclude—conclusion, express—expression, emit—emission, omit—omission
-ment	develop—development, punish—punishment, employ—employment, achieve—achievement, arrange—arrangement, advertise—advertisement
-ence	depend—dependence, exist—existence, emerge—emergence, interfere—interference, persist—persistence
-ance	resist—resistance, resemble—resemblance, enter—entrance, ignore—ignorance
-ure	mix—mixture, press—pressure, expose—exposure
-al	arrive—arrival, survive—survival, remove—removal, withdraw—withdrawal, deny—denial
-ity	able—ability, similar—similarity, responsible—responsibility, diverse—diversity, formal—formality
-ness	aware—awareness, dark—darkness, careless—carelessness, conscious—consciousness, useful—usefulness, thoughtful—thoughtfulness
-th	warm—warmth, deep—depth, long—length
-ery/-ry	bribe—bribery, rob—robbery, refine—refinery, bake—bakery
-ship	friend—friendship, leader—leadership, hard—hardship
-ism	criticize—criticism, realize—realism

A typical nominal group is structured with nominalizations functioning as its head, which can be pre-modified or post-modified prepositional phrases introduced by "of". For example：

(1) ST：Rectification of this fault is achieved by insertion of a wedge.

TT：嵌入一个楔子就可以纠正误差。

(2) ST：Archimedes first discovered the principle of displacement of water by solid bodies.

TT：阿基米德最先发现固体排放水的原理。

(3) ST：Reduced consumption of meat, increased use of new high-protein food made from soybeans, and development of ocean resources for food are some alternatives that must be considered.

TT：减少肉类消费,更多地食用大豆制的高蛋白食品,开发海洋食品资源,都是必须予以考虑的方案。

Chapter Two Contrastive Study Between English and Chinese

(4) ST: Efficient utilization of these waste materials can convert them into useful products by such processes as recycling of the nutrients, replenishment of soil organic matter or generation of useful energy.

TT: 有效地利用这些废弃物可以将它们转化成有用的产品,比如说可以通过回收营养物质、填充土壤有机物,或生产可用能源等方式。

Sometimes associated with nominalization is the occurrence of prepositional phrases, introduced by *to*, *with*, *on*, *for*, etc. For example:

(1) ST: Another possibility is that exposure to the wider world via the Net makes users less satisfied with their lives.

TT: 另外一种可能是,网民通过互联网了解了广阔的世界。这使他们对自己的生活感到不满。

(2) ST: This includes familiarity with the spoken language and with body language; knowledge of the country's social customs and formalities; awareness of the degree to which subtleness or, inversely, directness is current in negotiations.

TT: 这包括熟悉他们的口语和肢体语言,了解该国的社会习俗和礼仪,意识到谈判过程中通行的含蓄或直率可以达到何种程度。

(3) ST: In talking to some scientists, particularly younger ones, you might gather the impression that they find the "scientific method" a substitute for imaginative thought.

TT: 在和一些科学家,尤其是年轻的科学家交谈的时候,你或许会得出这一印象:他们认为"科学的方法"可以取代发散思维。

(4) ST: Samsung has established a firm grip on the mobile spectrum by launching several spectacular handsets into the competitive mobile market.

TT: 三星向竞争激烈的移动通讯市场投放了数款引人注目的手机,从而牢牢掌握了移动通信频谱资源。

(5) ST: The lack of goods, services, and household aids, brought on by the country's concentration on heavy industry at the expense of consumer goods, affects women much more than men.

TT: 国家重视重工业,忽视消费品生产,由此带来的商品、服务设施和家用电器的短缺对女士的影响要比对男士的大。

There are two ways in E-C translation of such nouns. One way is to translate them into nouns, and the other way is to convert them into verbs as is shown in the above examples. The following are more examples:

(1) ST: The manufacture of goods and the preparation of foodstuffs depend upon the availability of a vast source of mechanical power.

TT: 货物生产和食物储备依靠机械能量。

(2) ST: Reliability and maintainability characteristics are the two most critical features of equipment which influence the total cost of maintenance and also its management. (Uday Kumar: Maintenance management for modern mining equipment)

TT：设备的可靠性和可维修性是设备的两个最重要的特点，不仅会影响设备的总维修费用，还会影响设备的维修管理。

（3）ST：The enhancement of educational exchanges and cooperation will help us all to learn from one another's experiences and overcome our problems and deficiencies.

TT：加强我们两国以及各国的教育交流与合作，将起到互相学习、借鉴、取长补短的作用。

（4）ST：To assist in the examination, evaluation and comparison of bids, the Employer and A Company may request bidders individually for clarification of their bids.

TT：为了帮助检查、评价和比较标书，业主和 A 公司可要求投标者就其标书做出解释。

（5）ST：I enjoy the closeness to nature that the rehabilitation process required.

TT：我喜欢接近大自然。这是恢复身体过程所需要的。

2.6　English Passive Voice and Its Translation

Passive voice is commonly used in English, which even becomes a habit in scientific and bureaucratic writing. S. Baker (1992:35) in his works *The Practical Stylist* states that "our massed, scientific, and bureaucratic society is so addicted to the impassive voice that you must constantly alert yourself against its drowsy, impersonal pomp". It is estimated that one third of the verbs in scientific text are in passive voice, in that scientists are much more interested in action and facts rather than actors, which seems to express result and findings more objectively and impersonally. However, in Chinese passive voice is not used frequently because it was considered an unlucky voice in tradition (Lian, 2000). The following are some commonly used methods to translate English passive sentences.

2.6.1　Translating into active voice by keeping the original subject

（1）ST：Many old houses were pulled down, and many new ones were built in their places.

TT：许多老房子拆了，新房子就在原地盖起来了。

（2）ST：No matter which acids or bases are mixed, the chemical reaction also forms water.

TT：无论何种酸碱物质混合在一起，所引起的化学反应都会产生水。

（3）ST：Manufacturing processes may be classified as unit production with small quantities being made and mass production with large numbers of identical parts being produced.

TT：制造方法可分为单件生产和批量生产，单件生产指小批量的生产，批量生产指大量相同零件的生产。

（4）ST：This product has been inspected before delivery and is in full conformity with our standard.

TT：本产品出厂前经检验,完全符合标准。

2.6.2　Translating into active voice by changing the original actor (adverbial) into subject

(1) ST：The mechanical energy can be changed back into electrical energy by means of a generator.

TT：发电机可以把机械能转换为电能。

(2) ST：Even when the hours of light stay the same, changes in atmospheric temperature can be caused by air flow.

TT：即使光照时间不变,空气的流动也能引起气温的变化。

(3) ST：The advent of numerical control was predicted by many to be the end of coping.

TT:许多人曾经预言数控技术的出现将是仿形加工(工艺)的终结。

(4) ST：Atoms cannot be destroyed or changed in any way by chemical reactions.

TT：化学反应在任何情况下都无法破坏或改变原子。

2.6.3　Translating into active voice by adding a proper subject

(1) ST：Laser has been found efficient in drilling small holes.

TT:人们发现用激光钻小孔效率很高。

(2) ST：Few deep sea animals are known in their natural living.

TT：我们很少见到自然生存状态的深海生物。

(3) ST：Weak magnetic fields are known to come from the human body.

TT：我们知道人体能产生微弱的磁场。

(4) ST：The earth must be protected because it is our home.

TT：我们必须保护地球,因为它是我们的家园。

2.6.4　Translating into "是……的" for some descriptive or judgement sentences

(1) ST：The manuscript was sent to the printer in London a few weeks before the French Revolution.

TT:手稿是在法国大革命前几星期寄往伦敦复印的。

(2) ST：The volume is not measured in square millimeters, but in cubic millimeters.

TT：体积不是以平方毫米计量的,而是以立方毫米计量的。

(3) ST：Many mountains and large lakes are formed by the movement of the earth's crust.

TT：许多高山和大湖都是由于地壳运动形成的。

(4) ST：Concrete is made of cement, sand, stones and water.

TT:混凝土是由水泥、沙子、石子和水混合制成的。

(5) ST：The AIDS virus was found in human white blood cells in 1983.

TT：艾滋病病毒<u>是</u> 1983 年在人体白细胞内发现<u>的</u>。

(6) ST：This kind of device is much needed in the mechanical watch-making industry.

TT：这种装置在机械钟表制造业中<u>是</u>急需<u>的</u>。

2.6.5 Translating into active voice with no subject

(1) ST：With a gear reduction, the output speed can be reduced while the torque is increased.

TT：如果使用齿轮减速，就可以降低输出速度，同时增加力矩。

(2) ST：Acceptance and shipment of the products shall be discontinued until corrective action has been taken.

TT：在采取正确措施之前，应该暂停产品的验收和装运。

(3) ST：Great efforts should be made to inform young people the dreadful consequences of taking up the habit of smoking.

TT：应尽最大努力告诫年轻人吸烟上瘾后的可怕后果。

(4) ST：Methods are found to take these materials out of the rubbish and use them again.

TT：已经找到了从垃圾中提取这些材料并加以利用的方法。

(5) ST：Account should be taken of the low melting point of this substance.

TT：应该考虑这种物质的熔点低。

(6) ST：The solar energy can be converted into electrical energy by using solar panels.

TT：利用太阳能板可以将太阳能转化成电能。

2.6.6 Translating into Chinese passive sentences by using "被……""给……"
　　　　"叫……""遭……""受……""为……所""加以""予以"，etc.

(1) ST：In that work, light pulses <u>were technically "stored"</u> briefly when individual particles of light, or photons, <u>were taken up</u> by atoms in a gas.

TT：在试验中，单个的光粒子或光子在某种气体中<u>被</u>原子接纳时，光脉冲很快<u>被</u>巧妙地"<u>储存</u>"起来。

(2) ST：The moment contact is made, the free electrons of the conductor <u>are forced</u> to drift toward the positive terminal under the influence of field.

TT：导体一旦接触，其自由电子在磁场的影响下<u>被</u>迫向正极漂移。

(3) ST：After several years of hard work, Mr. Smith <u>was appointed</u> as editorial director.

TT：经过多年的努力，史密斯先生<u>被</u>任命为编辑部主任。

(4) ST：North China <u>was hit</u> by an unexpected heavy rain, which caused severe flooding.

TT：华北地区<u>遭受</u>了一场意外的大雨袭击，引起了严重的水灾。

(5) ST：Nuclear weapons plants across the country <u>are heavily contaminated</u> with toxic

Chapter Two　Contrastive Study Between English and Chinese

wastes.

TT：全国的核武器工厂均<u>受到了</u>有毒废弃物的严重<u>污染</u>。

（6）ST：The doctor is greatly respected by people because of his medical skill and kindness.

TT：这个医生妙手仁心，因而<u>深受</u>大家的<u>尊重</u>。

（7）ST：The problem <u>can be solved</u> in all manner of ways.

TT：这个问题可以用各种方法<u>加以</u>解决。

2.6.7　Translating the fixed structure "It＋is＋past participle that..."

It is reported that... 据报道……

It is supposed that... 据推测……

It must be admitted that... 必须承认……

It will be seen that... 由此可见……

It is asserted that... 有人主张……

It is believed that... 有人相信……

It is generally considered that... 大家普遍认为……

It is well-known that... 众所周知……

...

The following are some examples demonstrating the methods of translation.

（1）ST：<u>It is believed</u> to be natural that more and more engineers have come to prefer synthetic material to natural material.

TT：愈来愈多的工程人员宁愿用合成材料而不用天然材料。<u>人们相信</u>这是很自然的。

（2）ST：<u>It is believed</u> that fever and the conditions that accompany it are protective reactions to overcome the effect of toxins on the body.

TT：<u>人们相信</u>，发烧及其伴随的症状是人体克服毒素效应的保护性反应。

（3）ST：<u>It is strongly advised</u> that you take out insurance.

TT：<u>奉劝</u>你务必办理保险。

（4）ST：<u>It has been known</u> for many years that wireless waves travel at very great speeds.

TT：许多年以来<u>人们就已经知道</u>，无线电传播的速度极快。

（5）ST：<u>It is commonly asserted that</u> older people prefer to receive care from family members.

TT：<u>人们普遍断定</u>，老年人更愿意被家人照顾。

（6）ST：<u>It is well known</u> that Albert Einstein was one of the greatest scientists of all time.

TT：<u>众所周知</u>，阿尔伯特·爱因斯坦是有史以来最伟大的科学家之一。

（7）ST：<u>It must be admitted that</u> the theoretical economics study of the editorial economics has some shortcomings, so the relative study should follow certain scientific principles in order to make a further development.

TT：必须承认，经济编辑学的理论研究还存在明显不足，相关的研究还必须遵循一定的科学原则深入进行。

2.6.8 Translating passive voice into other structures

In some cases, however, the passive voice in English cannot be rendered into good Chinese by any of the above means. Therefore, it is up to the translator to adjust or remold the whole structure, trying to find a readable and smooth Chinese version. For example：

(1) ST：The village is populated by about 13,000 farmers.

TT：这个村子里住着大约 13 000 位农民。

(2) ST：The news was passed on by word of mouth.

TT：众口相传，消息不胫而走。

(3) ST：He has been wedded to history study.

TT：他与历史研究结下了不解之缘。

(4) ST：Many factors are involved in the combat effectiveness of submarines.

TT：涉及潜艇战斗力的因素很多。

(5) ST：Whoever eats it will be blessed.

TT：谁吃了谁就有福。

In brief, we have done a systematic contrastive study between English and Chinese from aspects of linguistic code to communicative conventions. The findings can provide some implications for foreign language teaching, learning and translation.

Chapter Three Translation of Tourism Promotional Texts

Tourism has become an important economic field in many parts of the world. With the development of globalization and accelerating mobility in the twenty-first century, the tourism industry is more flourishing than ever before. International tourist arrivals have increased from merely 278 million globally in 1980 to 1.3 billion in 2017 (UNWTO, 2018: 2) and reach 1.4 billion by 2021. The ever-increasing number of tourists worldwide has turned the tourism industry into one of the fastest-growing economic sectors in the world and a key driver of socio-economic progress. The tourism industry has also witnessed the proliferation of a huge range of tourism products with different labels for different settings, environments and experiences.

In recent years, tourism has become an important field for the study of intercultural communication and translation. It is often the case that international visitors receive their first impression of a country from the translation of tourism promotional texts, be it a brochure, a leaflet or a website (Kelly, 1998: 34).

3.1 Definition of Tourism Promotional Texts

Tourism promotional texts (TPTs) are a form of advertising texts in the field of marketing and advertising (Middleton et al., 2009: 316). They are described as the collection of media, such as brochures, leaflets, posters, flyers, postcards and websites, used to support the sales of tourism products. TPTs come in a variety of formats ranging from print to online materials. One of the most important and widely used TPTs to promote travel destinations is the tourist brochure. The tourist brochure may contain detailed written information on the tourism product. The aim of tourism advertising is to create perceptions, beliefs, impressions, ideas and expectations that satisfy a need in the mind of the potential tourist. Such advertisements are likely to trigger an appealing image of the destination, and leading to a certain degree of motivational intensity within the consumer to satisfy his/her needs by purchasing the tourism product (Horenberg, 2015: 11).

3.2　Functions of the TPTs

Based on Katharina Reiss's(1989: 105 - 115) text typology, TPTs are considered operative or persuasive texts. Their dominant function is to induce behavioral responses, by persuading, attracting attention and arousing interest. The readers are called upon to buy a holiday, to travel to a tourist destination, to become tourists. However, despite their dominant operative function, TPTs also convey essential information and are therefore informative and content-oriented (Snell-Hornby, 1999: 96). The expressive function is also evident in TPTs in the sense that they often rely on distinctly expressive elements (e. g. figurative languages) in order to communicate thoughts in a creative manner and create the intended effect (Snell-Hornby, 1999:96). In other words, TPTs depend on the interplay of all three textual functions (operative, informative and expressive) to achieve their purpose. However, it is the persuasive-informative mix in particular that has attracted the attention of a number of scholars. Sanning (2010: 125) describes the operative function as the goal and the informative function as the premise. He maintains that the persuasive function of TPTs is achieved through the provision of sufficient background information (informative function). An accurate, adequate and attractive description of the tourism product will strengthen the potential tourist's resolve to purchase the product. In this respect, the function of TPTs is two fold: to persuade potential tourists and provide them with information (Kelly, 1998: 35). Based on these two important functions, Prieto Arranz (2005:113) and Valdeón (2009: 21) describe TPTs as "info-promotional" materials. Snell-Hornby (1999:100) describes TPMs as materials that present a more or less balanced blend of information and persuasion through words and images.

3.3　Differences Between English and Chinese TPTs

In many cases, advertising and promotional materials are translated "too literally" leading to communication problems. As a result, these translations become barriers rather than aids to success (Anholt, 2000: 273 - 275). One of the problems in the translation of TPTs is perhaps the assumption that TPTs are a universal genre with universal norms and conventions across languages and cultures. However, research in translation studies has shown that the genre conventions of tourism promotion differ significantly from one language to another. In fact, people communicate and respond to communication messages based on their own cultural norms, rules and values which form the basis for preferred communication styles. These communication styles define how one should communicate and how communication messages should be taken, interpreted, filtered or understood. Therefore, knowing the strategies and conventions of the language of tourism promotion in the target language is essential. The knowledge of the difference is undoubtedly useful for formulating translation strategies, which can make the TPTs translator a cross-cultural transcreator.

3.3.1 Characteristics of Chinese TPTs

1. Poetic style of writing

Many Chinese writers of scenic descriptions, influenced by Chinese literary tradition, seem to be fond of lyrical writing, pursuing rhythmical prose styles, well-proportioned parallel structures and elaborate descriptions. As a result, many Chinese tourism texts are characterized by grandiose diction and abundant adjectives and four-character phrases (Chinese *Chengyu*). These poetic devices are used as a tool of emphasis to attract the reader's attention and imprint the message in the mind of the reader.

Example 1

武夷山有三十六峰,七十二洞,九十九岩,由红色沙砾岩层叠而成。群峰秀拔奇伟,千姿百态;溪水澄碧清澈,绕峰回旋。雨过初晴,山岚飘忽,彩虹飞渡,碧水映丹山,丹山转碧水,游人置身其中,宛入人间仙境。

This is a description of Mount Wuyi taken from a travel brochure, which reflects typical features of Chinese tourism texts. In this short introduction of only 95 Chinese characters, nine four-character phrases or idioms are employed to achieve rhythm and parallelism. This superfluous writing style is typical of Chinese scenic descriptions which depict a vivid picture in Chinese reader's mind. The following are more examples:

Example 2

苏州位于沪宁线上,地处太湖之滨,建成于公元前415年,是我国江南著名的古老城市之一。城内外遍布名胜古迹。寒山寺,诗韵钟声,脍炙人口;虎丘,千年古塔,巍然屹立;太平山,奇石嶙峋,枫林如锦;洞庭东山,湖光山色,花果连绵。

Example 3

进入山中,重峦叠嶂,古木参天;峰回路转,云断桥连,涧深谷幽,天光一线,灵猴嬉戏,琴蛙奏弹;奇花铺径,别有洞天。春季万物萌动,郁郁葱葱;夏季百花争艳,姹紫嫣红;秋季红叶满山,五彩缤纷;冬季银装素裹,白雪皑皑。(武夷山)

The above examples reveal that Chinese tend to adopt a literary style with extensive use of figurative language to impress and attract readers and create a favorable image in the mind of the consumers. The parallel structure and four-word set phrases act as "verbal charms" which create a spell effect on the readers.

However, English speaking people are likely to reject this kind of writing, regarding it to be too exaggerating and repetitive. Therefore, if translators render TPTs literally from Chinese into English, it may lead to confusion or redundancy for western readers, for whom this violates the convention of TPTs in their culture.

2. Elaborate evaluation of tourist spots

Many Chinese tourist brochures make elaborate evaluation of scenic spots or overstate them so as to impress readers.

Example 1

九寨沟位于四川省阿坝藏族羌族自治州九寨沟县境内,是白水沟上游白河的支沟,以有九个藏族村寨(所以又称何药九寨)而得名。九寨沟海拔在两千米以上,遍布原始森林,沟内分布一百零八个湖泊,有"<u>童话世界</u>"之誉;九寨沟为全国重点风景名胜区,并被列入<u>世界遗产名录</u>。2007年5月8日,阿坝藏族羌族自治州九寨沟旅游景区经国家旅游局正式批准为<u>国家5A级旅游景区</u>。

This brief introduction of Jiuzhai Valley emphasizes its status as a tourist spot in China and people's impressions about it. Lexical items such as "童话世界", "世界遗产名录", and "国家5A级旅游景区" to be chosen with utmost care, as they can reflect the glowing qualities of the destination (e.g. fascinating, extraordinary and unique). More importantly, they must be able to fire the motivation of the tourists by complying with their expectations.

Example 2

秦始皇兵马俑博物馆位于陕西省西安市临潼区秦陵镇,成立于1975年11月,原为秦始皇兵马俑筹建处,于1979年10月1日正式开馆,建于临潼区(原临潼县)东7.5千米的骊山北麓的秦始皇帝陵兵马俑坑遗址上,西距西安37.5千米;和骊山园合称秦始皇帝陵博物院。截至2020年1月,秦始皇兵马俑博物馆已接待海内外观众达8 000多万人次。秦兵马俑地下大军先后接待观众近5 000万人次,其中共接待外国国家元首、政府首脑187批,副总统、副总理和议长506批、部长级客人1 852批。

截至2020年1月,已先后建成并开放了秦俑一、三、二号坑和文物陈列厅。目前秦俑博物馆面积已扩大到46.1公顷,拥有藏品5万余(套)件。一号兵马俑坑内约埋藏陶俑、陶马6 000件,同时还有大量的青铜兵器;二号兵马俑坑内埋藏陶俑、陶马1 300余件,二号俑坑较一号俑坑的内容更丰富,兵种更齐全;三号俑坑的规模较小,坑内埋藏陶俑、陶马72件;陈列厅内有一、二号铜车马。

秦始皇兵马俑博物馆先后被评为全国文化系统先进集体、全国文博系统先进集体、全国精神文明建设先进单位,并荣获"全国五一劳动奖状"。秦始皇兵马俑博物馆为首批国家5A级旅游景区、首批国家一级博物馆。(百度百科)

In this example, the last paragraph is the evaluation of the spot to emphasize its fames and honors to attract readers.

3. Quotation of poems, famous people's remarks, anecdotes

In TPTs, classical Chinese literary works such as ancient poems, couplets, proverbs and the like are often cited to highlight the beauty or popularity of the tourist sites. These citations can not only enrich the historical and cultural connotations of the spots, but also enhance its aesthetic value.

Example 1

白云洞位于鼓山西北风池山西侧,海拔700多米,常常是"白云混入,咫尺莫辨",于是被称为"白云洞"。文人郁达夫游览白云洞后写道:"<u>一般人所说的白云洞的奇峰险路,果然是名不虚传的绝境</u>。"保证你去过一次,就会毕生也忘不了,妙处就在于它的险峻。

The description of Bai yun Cave quotes an appraisal of the scenic spot written by the famous Chinese contemporary writer Yu Dafu, so as to give readers the impression that this place is highly appreciated by well-known people and worth visiting. Usually, historical records, literature works, and positive remarks by famous people are favored by Chinese tourism texts writers when introducing a place of interest. These quotations are used to produce deep impressions on Chinese visitors. This point can be further illustrated by the following examples.

Example 2

花径公园是庐山旅游景点的一颗明珠,唐朝大诗人白居易在此游览时曾写下:"<u>人间四月芳菲尽,山寺桃花始盛开。长恨春归无觅处,不知转入此中来。</u>"的著名诗句。园内有白居易堂、觅春园、孔雀馆等参观项目,是集山水、人文、古代、现代为一体的综合性公园。

Example 3

泰山古称岱山,又称岱宗,位于山东省中部,为中国五岳(泰山、华山、衡山、嵩山、恒山)之一。因地处东部,故称东岳。泰山总面积 426 平方千米,主峰玉皇顶海拔 1 532.8 米,山势雄伟壮丽,气势磅礴,名胜古迹众多,有"五岳独尊"之誉。孔子有"<u>登泰山而小天下</u>"之语,唐朝大诗人杜甫有"<u>会当凌绝顶,一览众山小</u>"的佳句。泰山在人们的心目中,已成为伟大、崇高的象征。

Example 4

在我国最早的典籍中即有这条河的记载。《尚书·禹贡》:"漆沮既从,沣水攸同",《诗经·大雅》:"沣水东注,维禹之绩",说明沣水在远古就是一条著名的河流。

China is famous for its rich cultural resources, long history, numerous historical allusions, and classical literature which have become a valuable cultural legacy. In the above examples, each quotation gives a deep impression to its readers, which is both authentic and instructive. Therefore, in tourism literature, Chinese writers tend to cite such poems, celebrities' remarks, and anecdotes to develop shared connections with readers.

Nevertheless, if translated into English literally, many citations may lose their cultural connotations, and seem meaningless to foreign readers, so adaptation or paraphrase method should be adopted to deal with this issue.

4. Low frequency of using the second person pronoun

In terms of style, Chinese TPTs tend to be more formal, establishing a distant relationship with the reader who is seldom addressed directly. In other words, the degree of formality is reflected in the avoidance of the use of the second person pronoun "你"(you). Instead, Chinese writer usually uses "the visitor" or "the traveler" to address the reader, as is shown in the following examples.

Example 1

华山以其峻峭吸引了无数游<u>人</u>。山上的观、院、亭、阁皆依山势而建,一山飞峙,恰似空中楼阁,而且有古松相映,更是别具一格。山峰秀丽,又形象各异,如似韩湘子赶牛、金蟾戏龟、白蛇遭难……

Example 2

若<u>游人</u>投食入溪,鲤鱼欢腾跳跃,争相逐食。<u>游人</u>以手触鱼,温顺如驯,一幅天然的人鱼问乐图,显得格外亲近温馨。

In the above TPTs, the reader is involved in a more indirect and implicit manner, which is executed primarily by emphasizing the destination rather than the reader. Therefore, tourists in general and not the reader in particular are emphasized by means of third person referencing or by omitting.

5. Topic-prominent and paratactic sentence patterns

As is discussed in Chapter Two, topic predominant or theme-rhreme sentence is very common in descriptive writing such as the description of a person, a book, a scenery spot or an object which places more emphasis on the theme. Moreover, Chinese tourism texts are characterized by paratactic structure. Sentences are composed of independent clauses which are presented in chronologic order or logic without adopting linking words such as conjunctions, prepositions, relative connectives, etc. Some examples are listed as follows.

Example 1

山西省五台山是闻名中外的佛教圣地,境内迄今为止仍保存着北魏、唐、宋、元、明、清及民国等历朝历代的寺庙建筑47座。精美绝伦的古代建筑、稀世文物及博大精深的佛教文化充满了无限的神秘感。

Example 2

千佛山是泰山的余脉,东西绵亘,翠峰连绵,重峦叠嶂,松柏翁郁,犹如济南的一道天然屏障。

It is clear that the topic "山西省五台山" in Example 1 and "千佛山" in Example 2 refer to the theme or the topic of the text that the speaker will discuss. The rest of the sentences following the topics are further explanations, comments, and evaluations of the tourist spots. They are all used to emphasize the topic. In addition, the sentence structures are quite loose with fewer connectives are used to link each part.

3.3.2 Characteristics of English TPTs

Unlike its Chinese counterpart, English TPTs put more emphasis on practical information such as specific spots, activities, facilities, etc. The language tends to be less formal so as to establish direct communication with the reader by using first and second person forms and colloquial appealing languages (Kelly, 1998: 36).

1. Highly informative with plain language

The English writers describe the scenery in a down-to-earth way by focusing on providing exact and necessary information about tourist spots such as the environment, facilities, activities, tips and warnings, etc. They do not use as much superfluous description as Chinese do. Instead, they prefer plain and concise language.

Example 1

Grand Canyon, Arizona

The great gorge is accessible from two sides, north and south. Most of more than five million visitors per year choose to go to the South Rim, which has many more tourist facilities than the north side and, accordingly, tends to get action-packed during the summer season and even some winter weekends. The North Rim is a quieter and more remote place and preferred by people who wish for a more serene, less crowded experience.

The access road to the North Rim is frequently closed during winter due to snow. Both rims can get very cold in the winter, and nights are cool even during summer months. Hiking inside the canyon below the rim, however, is quite another story, as summer temperatures near the Colorado River at the bottom may reach 120 degrees Fahrenheit. Hikers, in particular, will face extreme changes in climate and should be prepared for these.

Example 2

Hoover Dam

The Hoover Dam is one of Nevada's proudest possessions. It displaces the Colorado River and creates Lake Mead, a large man-made waterway. You'll find a delicious meal at one of the many restaurants found within the Lake Mead National Recreation Area. At night, try the Lake Mead Cruise for dinner and dancing, as well as beautiful scenery. There is even a nearby theater, the Regal Boulder Station, that shows contemporary films.

From the above examples, we can see that the English TPTs pay much attention to offer substantial information such as what to see, what to do, time to visit, traffic, challenges, warnings, and so on. They do not exaggerate on the feelings or comments of the writers by avoiding too many descriptions.

2. Application of specific adjectives to show novelty and strangeness of the spots

The most frequently used technique in English TPTs are the frequent application of empathic and euphoric words to create an image of pleasure, excitement, novelty and authenticity. Specific lexical items such as "primitive", "natural", "different", "colourful", "exotic", "unique", "remote", "timeless", "traditional", "original", "real", "actual", "enticing", "glorious", "picturesque", "stunning", "magical", "wonderful", "breath-taking", "perfect", "spectacular", "untouched", "unspoilt", "amusing" and the alike are often used to describe tourist spots to enhance the paradisiac image and the pristine beauty.

Example 1

On the road leading to Central Europe to Adriatic coast lies a small Slovenian town of Postojna. Its subterranean world holds some of Europe's most magnificent underground galleries. Time losses all meanings in the formation of these underground wonders. Dripstones, stalactites, in different shapes—columns, pillars and translucent curtains, conjure up unforgettable images.

Example 2

The Washington Cathedral was constructed by traditional methods used by crafts people from Europe over the centuries. It is gothic in design and the details of its construction are readily available at the Cathedral. It is a functioning church, with several chapels below the main level. The stained glass windows are unique and each tells a story. The grounds of the cathedral are well maintained and there are many <u>quiet</u> spots for contemplation and enjoyment of the view as <u>the highest</u> point in the District of Columbia. The Cathedral Gift shop and the Herb Cottage Gift shop are well worth a visit.

Example 3

The Maasai Mara is one of the <u>best-known</u> reserves in the whole of Africa, and is globally renowned for its <u>exceptional</u> wildlife. Despite comprising only 0.01% of Africa's total landmass, more than 40% of Africa's <u>larger</u> mammals can be found here. Across the <u>vast</u> plains of the Mara, visitors are able to witness lions, cheetahs, leopards, elephants, and an infinite variety of other species in their natural habitats.

The Maasai Mara lies in the Great Rift Valley, which is a fault line some 3,500 miles (5,600 km) long stretching from Ethiopia's Red Sea through Kenya, Tanzania, Malawi, and into Mozambique. Here the valley is wide, and a <u>towering</u> escarpment can be seen in the hazy distance. The animals are at liberty to move outside the park into <u>huge</u> areas known as "dispersal areas". There can be as much wildlife roaming outside the park as inside. Many Maasai villages are located in the "dispersal areas" and they have, over centuries, developed a <u>synergetic</u> relationship with the wildlife.

Mara and Serengeti parks are <u>interdependent</u> wildlife havens. This is where the world's <u>largest</u> multi-species migration takes place. The movement is, centered around the wildebeest migrating from Serengeti into Masai Mara during the dry period in Tanzania, crossing the <u>mighty</u> Mara River on their way.

In the above examples, the use of the underlined lexical items creates an image of fun, beauty, uniqueness and specialty which participants adore.

Furthermore, the language of tourism promotion does not reflect what is average or normal, which makes it a form of extreme language. This "extremism" is also reflected in the use of emphasizers and superlative forms (*the highest*, *largest*, *proudest*) to evoke the motivational themes and fire the imagination of the readers.

3. Ego-targeting

Ego-targeting (Francesconi, 2007: 103) is a strategy used to maintain communication link with the reader throughout the host-tourist "conversation". The "conversation" exploits first-person and second-person pronouns such as "you", "we", "your" and "our". This strategy creates a friendship-like relationship between the host and the potential tourist, thus reducing any barrier the reader may have erected (Maci, 2007: 60).

Example 1

The Glacier Express cuts a cross-section through stunning Switzerland—pure train-travel pleasure. Prepare to be pampered in the Glacier Express. Savour meals specially prepared by <u>our</u> chef served in <u>our</u> stylish dining car. Or relax in <u>your</u> comfortable seat and enjoy coffee, snacks and drinks served from <u>our</u> minibar. The Glacier-Express is superb in all four seasons: shimmering peaks in summer, snow-covered, fairy-tale scenery in winter, fabulous Alpine flowers in spring and a kaleidoscope of color in autumn.

Example 2

In the afternoon, you can explore the city by bicycle—and the fact that bikes for both adults and children can be rented for free makes this method of transportation more fun. Bikes are available all year round from Velogate by the Swiss National/Museum and, from May to October, from outside Globs, the opera House and Swissotel Oerlikon.

Example 3

Learn about Australia's culture, history and way of life in our nation's capital. Explore our political past and modern democracy at the Museum of Australian Democracy and Parliament House. Find out more about our sporting heroes at the National Institute of Sport and Science and experience an earthquake at Questacon. Once you've exhausted the monuments and galleries, get into the great outdoors. This culturally-rich capital is famous for its lake, parklands and native bushland surrounds. Beneath the foliage, Canberra offers stylish restaurants, hip bars, boutique shopping and a non-stop calendar of festivals and events.

From the above examples, we can see that the use of the first-person and second-person pronouns are compelling because there is a gradual shift of focus from tourists in general to the reader (you). And also, there is a gradual shift of focus from the destination to the reader (you). This is the most direct way to persuade the reader as it shortens the distance between the author and the reader and creates an illusion of friendship and familiarity.

4. Subject-predicate and hypotactic sentence structure

Unlike Chinese, the core structure of the English sentence is subject-predicate no matter how long the sentence is. In addition, there are many complex sentences that normally consist of one main clause and some subordinate clauses. These long sentences are often linked by conjunctions and prepositions. What's more, relative pronouns or relative adverbs are used to connect the main clause and its subordinate clause.

Example 1

Now owned by Six Continents Hotels, the name Holiday Inn goes from strength to strength. It's the choice of millions including politicians and pop stars, because they know its name is a reassurance of a global standard of value and quality. Holiday Inn has a fascinating history and a fantastic future, because they still know what people want, and they still offer more than expected. That's why they continue to be the number one choice around the world. They're the world's most popular hotel chain, and their popularity just keeps growing. They know how to make guests feel welcome and they're known for their call-do service—if there's anything we can do to enhance your stay, we will. They're committed to giving you the best quality and value for money.

Reading this advertisement of the Holiday Inn, we can notice that the structure of all sentences is subject-predicate, and connectives such as "and" "if", "because", relative pronoun "it", "they" are used to link different parts of the sentence.

Example 2

Las Vegas Recommended Tours

Las Vegas may be known as the "sin city", but it has a lot of great attractions. Certainly, the casinos and nightlife are what bring visitors here, but there are so much more to do. There are several historic and interesting sites that are perfect for guided or self-guided tours.

The Hoover Dam is one of Nevada's proudest possessions. It displaces the Colorado River and creates Lake Mead, a large man-made waterway. You'll find a delicious meal at one of the many restaurants found within the Lake Mead National Recreation Area. At night, try the Lake Mead Cruise for dinner and dancing as well as beautiful scenery. There is even a nearby theater, the Regal Boulder Station that shows contemporary films.

This is also a typical English TPTs with a subject-predicate sentence structures and hypotatic features by using different connective devices such as conjunctions "but", "as well as", relative pronouns "that", and pronouns "it".

As is mentioned above, English and Chinese TPTs display distinctive stylistic patterns which correspond to the cultural characteristics of the readership. Different stylistic features have different functions and create different effects in different cultural contexts. Therefore, translation must be guided by the genre conventions of TPTs in the target language and the overall purpose for which the translation is intended.

3.4 Principles for Tourism Translation

In TPTs translation, it is not language in its linguistic forms but rather language in its cultural context that creates meaning in people's mind. The translation of tourism advertising discourse is an act of recreating meaning and effect using a different language that operates in a different cultural framework. In TPTs translation, three non-linguistic principles have been identified as crucial: agility, persuasiveness and creativity.

Agility is the "ability to recognize different functions and purposes embedded in the source text, and deal with them appropriately without losing sight of the overall function of the text" (Torresi, 2010: 8). In TPTs translation, it is the persuasive and informative functions that are most crucial. Sumberg (2004: 342) points out that the failure of TPT translation is partly due to the fact that translators fail to distinguish between these two functions and therefore do not adopt appropriate techniques accordingly. Therefore, figuring out the average information-to-persuasion ratio of the TPT genre across different cultures is critical for the selection of appropriate translation strategies.

The second principle is persuasiveness which refers to the mastery of an emotional style which lures the audience into action because the function of TPTs is to capture attention, arouse interest, create desire and call for action. According to translation scholars Sumberg (2004: 334), the persuasiveness is central in TPT copywriting, it should also be an important strategy for TPT translators. The ultimate aim of this strategy is to mould the message in such a way so as to achieve the intended effects of persuading the reader to act. It must also be noted that this will only be possible by accommodating the culturally predicated needs and preferences of the readers.

The third principle is creativity, which is the ability to be creative in the production of the translation. Translation creativity focuses on adapting someone else's ideas creatively and tailoring the text to the target culture to achieve the intended effects of persuading the target audience. The translator has to be able to think beyond the language and look at the greater picture: the conventional style of writing, the reader and the target culture. More importantly, the translator must not be confined by the source text and source culture, so a combination of interlinguistic translation and these three principles might be an ideal way to overcome cultural barriers in order to achieve the ultimate purpose of tourism advertising.

3.5 Functional Approach in TPTs Translation

Sumberg (2004: 343) who studied the quality of TPTs translation says that the poor standard of translated TPTs is attributed to the translation approach adopted. She claims that the adoption of a linguistic approach (which focuses on the linguistic features of the source text), rather than a functional one (which focuses on the function and purpose) is the main cause of the problem. As already noted, in the field of tourism advertising, the ultimate purpose is to turn a potential tourist into an actual tourist. Therefore, what becomes more important than fidelity to the linguistic features of the source text is the function in the target culture. The intended purpose of the target text, specific text-typological conventions, the intended audience and the socio-cultural context in the target text are the main concern in translation. This is in contrast with the traditional approach, which often view translation as "a reproduction of an existing source text, where 'the source text' is the main yardstick governing the translator's decision" (Nord, 2006:131). Instead, the source text is no longer the first and foremost criterion for the translator's decisions. It's just an "offer of information" (Reiss & Vermeer, 1984:67). Only those the translator regards as interesting, useful or adequate to the desired purposes are to be picked out and presented in a way that is supposed to be appropriate for target readers. In this model, the macro-level translation strategies determine the most effective micro-level techniques to be employed. In other words, the translator is able to make linguistic choices consonant with the target text's overall message. The micro-linguistic form is governed by macro-level factors, particularly, purpose and culture. Therefore, the translator has to select and process certain items from the source text in order to form a new offer of information in the target language. What items will be chosen and translated depends on the Skopos rule, and the selection should be able to give a meaningful rendition in the target culture, i. e. it should abide by the intratextual coherence rule.

3.6　C-E Translation of TPTs under the Guidance of Functional Approach

According to Skopos Theory, the key factor determining the choice of translating strategies is the purpose of the translation. In the case of TPTs, the ultimate purpose is to persuade, lure, woo and seduce readers, and convert them from potential into actual clients. Therefore, an effective translation strategy would be to translate these functions, not literally, but to recreate the favorable effects in the target language and culture. To reach the goal, the methods of paraphrasing, restructuring, rewriting, amplification and omission are often adopted.

3.6.1　Translating poetic descriptions

As is mentioned above, Chinese tourism texts prefer to use grandiose diction and abundant adjectives and four-character phrases (*Chengyu*). This style of writing is no doubt eloquent, descriptive and impressive for Chinese readers. However, it may seem exaggerating to the English readers who are used to the concise and informative tourism texts. They may regard this kind of text too pompous, verbose and confusing. If we translate the ST literally, it will violate the convention of its English counterpart, thus hindering the information delivery and function realization.

In this case, paraphrasing method is often adopted to render the flowery expressions in conformity with English norms. Paraphrasing is an effective way to retrieve the essential information from a sentence or text to express the meaning in other words for the purpose of clarification.

Example 1

ST：武夷山有三十六峰、七十二洞、九十九岩，由红色沙砾岩层叠而成。<u>群峰秀拔奇伟，千姿百态；溪水澄碧清澈，绕峰回旋。雨过初晴，山岚飘忽，彩虹飞渡，碧水映丹山，丹山转碧水</u>，游人置身其中，宛入人间仙境。

TT：Wuyi Mountain, which is composed of red gravel layers, has 36 peaks, 72 caves and 99 rocks. <u>The peaks are beautiful and magnificent with a variety of shapes and crystal clear stream circling around. After rain in sunny days, the mountain is more charming with the rainbow and flowing clouds around.</u> If you are here, you may feel you are in a fairyland.

Example 2

ST：苏州位于沪宁线上，地处太湖之滨，建成于公元前415年，是我国江南著名的古老城市之一。城内外遍布名胜古迹。<u>寒山寺，诗韵钟声，脍炙人口；虎丘，千年古塔，巍然屹立；太平山，奇石嶙峋，枫林如锦；洞庭东山，湖光山色，花果连绵。</u>

TT：Suzhou, located on the bank of Taihu Lake along the Shanghai-Nanjing Railway, is one of the famous ancient cities built in south China. It was built in 415 BC. There are many places of interest both inside and outside the city. <u>The famous ones include Hanshan Temple with a clear bell, Tiger Hill with a thousand-year-old pagoda, Taiping Mountain with rugged rocks and red maple trees and Dongting East Mountain with beautiful lakes, colorful flowers and various fruits.

Example 3

ST：桂林的山,平地拔起,百媚千娇,像高耸云霄的奇花巨葩,盛开在锦绣江南;漓江的水,澄明清澈,晶莹碧绿,恰似翡翠玉带,透逸于奇山秀峰之间。

TT：Guilin is surrounded by abrupt rock hills rising straight out of the ground. The hills have a myriad of forms, some graceful, others grotesque. Among them winds the flowing crystal green Lijiang River.

Analysis：In the above three examples, the beauty depicted by the heaps of adjectives and rhetorical devices in the original text gives way to the English plain style. The parallel structures and the four-words characters in the ST are not translated word for word. Instead, they are paraphrased to make the version more idiomatic to the English ears.

3.6.2 Translating elaborate evaluations

Many TPTs make elaborate evaluation of scenic spots or overstate them so as to impress readers and attract more visitors, which may sound verbose or even awkward in English.

Omission or omission plus compression is often used to deal with this issue. Omission refers to the deletion of certain words or expressions which don't conform to the thinking habits and expression habits of the target language. In other words, omission is the deletion of words or expressions which are unnecessary, burdensome, or contrary to the convention. While compression means to reduce or squeeze some redundant information to the right amount in the target language.

Example 1

ST：秦始皇兵马俑博物馆位于陕西省西安市临潼区秦陵镇,成立于 1975 年 11 月,于 1979 年 10 月 1 日正式开馆,建于临潼区(原临潼县)东 7.5 千米的骊山北麓的秦始皇帝陵兵马俑坑遗址上,西距西安 37.5 千米;和骊山园合称秦始皇帝陵博物院。截至 2020 年 1 月,秦始皇兵马俑博物馆已接待海内外观众达 8 000 多万人次。秦兵马俑地下大军先后接待观众近 5 000 万人次,其中共接待外国国家元首、政府首脑 187 批、副总统、副总理和议长 506 批、部长级客人 1852 批。

截至 2020 年 1 月,已先后建成并开放了秦俑一、三、二号坑和文物陈列厅。目前秦俑博物馆面积已扩大到 46.1 公顷,拥有藏品 5 万余(套)件。一号兵马俑坑内约埋藏陶俑、陶马 6 000 件,同时还有大量的青铜兵器;二号兵马俑坑内埋藏陶俑、陶马 1 300 余件,二号俑坑较一号俑坑的内容更丰富,兵种更齐全;三号俑坑的规模较小,坑内埋藏陶俑、陶马 72 件;陈列厅内有一、二号铜车马。

秦始皇兵马俑博物馆先后被评为全国文化系统先进集体、全国文博系统先进集体、全国精神文明建设先进单位,并荣获了"全国五一劳动奖状"。秦始皇兵马俑博物馆为首批国家 5A 级旅游景区、首批国家一级博物馆。(百度百科)

TT：Located in Lintong District, 37 kilometers west from Xi'an City, Shaanxi

Province, the Terracotta Warriors and Horses Museum was founded in November 1975 and officially opened on October 1, 1979. Built on the pit site of terracotta warriors and horses, together with the nearby Lishan Qinshihuang (the first emperor who united China) Mausoleum, it got its present name. By January 2020, the Museum has received more than 80 million visitors at home and abroad. <u>The underground army of Qin terracotta warriors and horses has received nearly 50 million visitors, including senior government leaders from different countries.</u>

By January 2020, pits 1, 3 and 2 of the terracotta warriors and the cultural relics exhibition hall have been completed and opened successively. At present, the area of the Museum of terracotta warriors has been expanded to 46.1 hectares, with a collection of more than 50,000 (sets). About 6,000 terra cotta warriors and horses as well as a large number of bronze weapons are buried in the No. 1 terra cotta pit. More than 1,300 terra cotta warriors and horses are buried in the No. 2 terra cotta pit. Compared with the No. 1 terra cotta pit, the No. 2 pit has richer contents and more types of soldiers. The size of No. 3 pit is small with 72 pottery figurines and horses buried. In the exhibition hall, copper cars and horses from No. 1 pit and No. 2 pit are displayed.

<u>With many honors and reputations, the Terracotta Warriors and Horses Museum of Qinshihuang is approved as the first batch of national 5A tourist attractions and the first batch of national first-class museums.</u>

Analysis: In the above example, in the first paragraph, <u>"秦兵马俑地下大军先后接待观众近 5 000 万人次,其中共接待外国国家元首、政府首脑 187 批,副总统、副总理和议长 506 批、部长级客人 1 852 批。"</u> is translated into "The underground army of Qin terracotta warriors and horses has received nearly 50 million visitors, <u>including senior government leaders from different countries.</u>" with "国家元首、政府首脑 187 批,副总统、副总理和议长 506 批、部长级客人 1 852 批" omitted and the information compressed.

And in the last paragraph, <u>"秦始皇兵马俑博物馆先后被评为全国文化系统先进集体,全国文博系统先进集体,全国精神文明建设先进单位,并荣获了"全国五一劳动奖状"</u> is compressed into "With many honors and reputations," by omitting the honors such as <u>"全国文化系统先进集体,全国文博系统先进集体,全国精神文明建设先进单位,并荣获了'全国五一劳动奖状'"</u>. The reason for omitting and compressing is that they carry little meaning or sound verbose to the English readers.

Example 2

ST:亚龙湾最突出、最引人入胜的是她的海水和沙滩。这里湛蓝的海水清澈如镜,能见度超过 10 米,海底珊瑚保存完整,生活着众多情态各异、色彩缤纷的热带鱼种,<u>是国家级珊瑚礁重点保护区</u>,因此也成了难得的潜水胜地。亚龙湾柔软细腻的沙滩洁白如银,延伸约 8 千米,长度约是美国夏威夷海滩的 3 倍。

TT: The most striking view of the Yalong Bay is the sea and beach. The sea water is clear with visibility as far down as 10 meters. Under the surface are well-protected coral reefs and all kinds of coral and colorful tropical fish, making it an ideal destination for divers. The beach is covered with silver-white sands extends 8 km, three times the length of the beach in Hawaii.

In this example,"是国家级珊瑚礁重点保护区，" is omitted, because it is redundant information in the text.

3.6.3　Translating quotation of poems, famous people's remarks and anecdotes

In Chinese TPTs, poems, celebrities' remarks, and anecdotes are often quoted to highlight the importance, beauty, or value of the tourist sites. Nevertheless, if translated into English literally, such citations seem meaningless to foreign readers who do not have the similar background knowledge, so omission ＋ paraphrasing method is adopted to deal with this issue.

Example 1

ST：花径公园是庐山旅游景点的一颗明珠，唐朝大诗人白居易在此游览时曾写下："人间四月芳菲尽，山寺桃花始盛开。长恨春归无觅处，不知转入此中来。"的著名诗句。园内有白居易堂、觅春园、孔雀馆等参观项目，是集山水、人文、古代、现代为一体的综合性公园。

TT：Huajing Park is a pearl of Lushan Mountain. Bai Juyi, a great poet of the Tang Dynasty, once wrote during his visit: "the flowers outside fell in April, while the peach blossoms in this mountain begin to bloom", which means people can come here to enjoy the spring beauty even in early summer. It is a comprehensive park integrating landscape, historic and cultural heritage of ancient and modern times with Bai Juyi Memorial, Spring-seeking Garden, Peacock Hall and other items.

Analysis: In the above example, poems are paraphrased because if the whole poem is omitted when translating, the translation would give inadequate information, for the quotation tries to tell people the beauty of the mountain in April.

Example 2

ST："烟水苍茫月色迷，渔舟晚泊栈桥西。乘凉每至黄昏后，人依栏杆水拍堤。"这是古人赞美青岛海滨的诗句。青岛是一座风光秀丽的海滨城市，夏无酷暑冬无严寒。西起胶州湾入海处的团岛，东至崂山风景区的下清宫，绵延80多华里的海滨组成了一幅绚烂多彩的长轴画卷。

TT：Qingdao is a beautiful coastal city. It is neither hot in summer nor cold in winter. The 40-km-long scenic line begins from Tuan Island at the west end and Xiaqing Gong of Mount Lao at the east end.

Analysis: In this example, the poem is deleted, because the meaning is expressed by the sentences following it.

Example 3

ST：在我国最早的典籍中，即有这条河的记载。《尚书·禹贡》："漆沮既从，沣水攸同"，《诗经·大雅》"沣水东注，维禹之绩"，说明沣水在远古就是一条著名的河流。

TT：Records about the river can be found even in the earliest Chinese classics thousands of years ago, which proves that the Feng River has been well known since ancient times.

Analysis: In this translation, the poems are omitted, because the poems are quoted in the ST just to prove that the river has a very long history. If translated, the version would become very verbose.

3.6.4 Transforming the third person pronoun to the second person pronoun

As is mention afore, Chinese writers tend to use "the visitor" or "the traveler" to address the reader in TPTs while the English prefer to using "you" to establish a close relationship with the reader. Therefore, in most cases, the translator should transform the third person pronoun to the second person pronoun to cater for the expectations, values and norms of the target readers.

Example:

ST: 若游人投食入溪,鲤鱼欢腾跳跃,争相逐食。游人以手触鱼,温顺如驯,一幅天然的人鱼同乐图,显得格外亲近温馨。

TT: If you throw food into the stream, the carps jump to compete for food. If you touch a carp with your hands, the carp is very gentle as if it was tamed, which forms a particularly warm and harmonious picture of people and carps.

3.6.5 Converting the Chinese topic-prominent sentence structure to English subject-predicate sentence structure

As is discussed in Chapter Two, topic-prominent sentences are prevalent in Chinese descriptive writing. However, such kind of information structure is not in line with the English subject-predicate structure. Therefore, the translator should make conversions in translation.

Example 1

ST: 山西省五台山是闻名中外的佛教圣地,境内迄今为止仍保存着北魏、唐、宋、元、明、清及民国历朝历代的寺庙建筑47座。精美绝伦的古代建筑、稀世文物及博大精深的佛教文化充满了无限的神秘感。

TT: Wutai Mountain, located in Shanxi Province, is a famous holy place of Buddhism. There remains 47 temples built from Northern Wei Dynasty (386 – 534) to the Republic of China(1912 – 1949). Exquisite ancient architecture, rare relics and splended Buddhism culture have all lent mystery to the mountain.

Analysis: the above topic-prominent Chinese sentences are translated into three English subject-predicate sentences.

Example 2

ST: 千佛山是泰山的余脉,东西绵亘,翠峰连绵,重峦叠嶂,松柏翁郁,犹如济南的一道天然屏障。

TT: Just like a natural screen protecting Jinan, the Thousand-Buddha Hill stretches from west to east with range upon range of mountains with verdant pine trees and cypresses.

Example 3

ST: 福建阳光假日大酒店是四星级涉外商务酒店,坐落于福州市中心,环境优越,交通便捷,独享 24 小时纯天然温泉。

TT: Sunshine Hotel is a four-star holiday inn located in the center of Fuzhou City with nice surroundings, convenient transport and 24-hour hot spring water.

3.6.5 Translating Chinese TPTs as a whole

Generally speaking, we do not take just one method to translate the TPTs. In most cases, comprehensive methods are adopted to deal with the more complicated situations.

Example 1

ST: 太乙·长安道景点介绍

一、项目简介

太乙·长安道旅游休闲小镇,南依终南,北眺渭水,白云青霭,秀丽旖旎。物华天宝,人杰地灵,福荫黎庶,名闻四方。诗与道交融称赞,水与山滋养膏腴。

项目传承数代教化之滥觞,坚持三生融合、四位一体发展理念,依托道家及中医养生文化、人文诗礼休闲文化、长安民俗文化内涵,以唐诗书法文化景观为轴,形成养生度假区、民俗娱乐区、文化休闲区三大板块,养生休闲街、养生膳食街、传统美食街、民优小吃街、历史文化街五大街区,太乙宫大殿、戏园、面食博物馆、茶园书院、养生阁、药膳坊等核心项目珠连玉串,共同建设成集休闲度假、养生养老、康体运动、创新创业、休闲娱乐、生态居住等功能为一体的旅游休闲小镇。以雕梁画壁为格调的仿古建筑,以中华中医养生、道教文化为特色,以养生膳食、中医保健、传统美食、民俗旅游、观光农业为基本业态。打造终南养生文化天堂,西北文化休闲旅游胜地。

二、景点介绍

1. 中国面食博物馆

中华面食文化历史悠久,八千年粟黍,四千年小麦。千百年来,淳朴厚道的中国人将希望与祈盼,通过灵巧的双手运用面食予以淋漓尽致地抒演。

诸葛亮七下南方祭水而馒头生,唐明皇求长寿乃有长寿面。

鸟献花馍,敬献春秋介子推;饺子多意,常来常往情谊深。

如馄饨之混沌初开,春卷之喜迎吉庆,婚嫁花糕,送客的饺子,从一物到百味,面食文化取法各地饮食文化,调理饮食生机,滋养饮食内涵。

中国面食博物馆,甄选实物图文,凝练面食精粹,将民族情结、节日风俗、人生礼仪,蕴含于一方面食天地,彰显面食文化之博大精深,积厚流光。

2. 戏园

尧舜净,汤武生,桓文丑旦,千古英雄收眼底;
日月灯,云霞彩,风雷鼓板,数声雅调在戏园。

在白云苍狗的历史长河里,岁月交替,繁华更迭,戏园都以旁观者的姿态展演人们对历史的敬畏与传承。

余音袅袅,丝弦声不绝如缕;
韵唱咿咿,看戏人超然忘我。

社区中央戏园,回廊相连,绿水为伴。西侧戏楼,东边影院,中为可供千人活动的文化广场。

老少居民,于此欢聚畅游,闲谈人生百事;艺人大家,于此呈现民俗民艺,传承中华文化精髓。

集体活动,文艺展演,众物共和,生活小天地,天地大舞台,生活与艺术在此水乳交融,墨守与交流在此合一共生。

3. 茶园书院

灵水仙饮,品一杯好茶,静看丰饶的人生。

琴韵墨香,读一本好书,知会物外的超然。

茶园书院,融中国传统文化与茶道文化研习,以数千年茶、道、艺为学养根基,修炼茶境、书境、意境,颐养雅致生活。

开辟安放心灵的家园,养生长寿的净土。

茶性清纯、质朴,书香淡雅、沉静,人性清虚、淡和,各方雅士名流于此汇集,喝赏心之茶,品悦目之书,修合一之境,茶烟琴韵书声里,无私无欲。

静守内心的平和、宁静、充实和自由,从容通达至逍遥。

偷得浮生半日闲,守护心灵清净圣地,喝茶读书,不争朝夕。

TT:Introduction to Taiyi · Chang'an Tao Recreation and Leisure Town

Ⅰ. Brief Introduction

Taiyi · Chang'an Tao, a tourist leisure town, is located at the foot of Zhongnan Mountain about 20 kilometers from Xi'an city. It is famous for its beautiful scenery, peaceful environment, rich natural resources, talented people, poetic atmosphere and Tao culture.

Inheriting several generations of wisdom of Taoism, traditional Chinese medicine, leisure culture, poetry and local folk culture, the town builds three main theme areas including health care part, folk entertainment part and leisure part with Tang poetry, calligraphy and cultural landscape. There are five streets: Health Care and Leisure Street, Healthy Dietary Street, Traditional Food Street, Snack Street, and Historical Street. The town is a recreation complex with Big Taiyi Hall, Theater, Pasta Museum, Tea House, Health Care Center and restaurants for people to spend their holidays, do physical exercises, and enjoy free time. The buildings in the town are featured with antique architecture of carved beams and walls. The town is designed as a holiday resort and leisure paradise for tourists in North-west China.

Ⅱ. Introduction to the Tourist Spots in the Town

1. Chinese Pasta Museum

Chinese pasta culture has a long history of thousands of years. Chinese people express their hopes and best wishes through pasta. The origin of steam buns, long noodles and dumplings are full of legends. *Wonton* indicates the beginning of the world; *Spring Roll* means the coming of a new year; flower cakes are made for weddings and noodles are cooked to welcome returning family members. Pasta is made with a hundred of different flavors and forms, which not only nurture the people, but also reflect the local culture.

In Chinese pasta museum, you can see the material objects and pictures of various pastas made by wheat and rice and feel the special customs and etiquette to have a better understanding of its real essence and profound culture values.

2. Theater

Here Chinese opera is performed every day. These operas tell the stories of Chinese history, heroic figures, great changes, romantic stories and common worldly life through vivid performance and beautiful singing. The audiences are often so indulged in the play that they feel they are part of the story.

The Central Theater is connected by a corridor and river with the opera tower in the west and cinema in the east. The cultural square in the center of the town can hold about a thousand of people for various activities. Artists demonstrate folk customs and arts to pass down the essence of Chinese culture. Collective activities and cultural performances are specially tailored for people of all ages. Art and life are blended harmoniously in this place.

3. Tea House with books

The tea house is a combination of tea culture, Taoism and arts. Here, you can drink a cup of good tea, read a book and feel the peace of mind. Sitting in the tea house to sip slowly, you can set the soul free, forget worries and anxiety, relax in the comfortable environment and enjoy the leisure time. The tea house not only attracts ordinary people, but also celebrities as well.

Analysis: Comparing the TT with ST, we can see that paraphrasing, omission plus compression, restructuring, amplification are combined to deliver the meaning and function of the ST.

Firstly, the complicated style of writing is reduced to a more concise way by omitting and compressing those excessive expressions which carry little substantial information such as "北眺渭水,白云青霭,秀丽旖旎。物华天宝,人杰地灵,福荫黎庶,名闻四方。诗与道交融称赞,水与山滋养膏腴。项目传承数代教化之滥觞,坚持三生融合、四位一体发展理念,依托道家及中医养生文化、人文诗礼休闲文化、长安民俗文化内涵", etc.

Secondly, paraphrasing is applied to translate some flowery expressions such as "尧舜净,汤武生,桓文丑旦,千古英雄收眼底;日月灯,云霞彩,风雷鼓板,数声雅调在戏园。在白云苍狗的历史长河里,岁月交替,繁华更迭,戏园都以旁观者的姿态展演人们对历史的敬畏与传承。余音袅袅,丝弦声不绝如缕;韵唱咿咿,看戏人超然忘我","灵水仙饮,品一杯好茶,静看丰饶的人生。琴韵墨香,读一本好书,知会物外的超然"。

Thirdly, restructuring is adopted to translate some paragraphs. Restructuring means necessary or inevitable change or adjustment of the word order or logic rearrangement of ST to make the version more smooth, readable and acceptable according to the expression habit of the TT readers. In this case, we adjust the logic order of the first point of Part Ⅱ (Ⅱ.1) from an inductive arrangement to deductive arrangement to highlight the topic "Chinese Pasta Museum".

Furthermore, second person pronoun is added when necessary to create an effect of close touch with the readers such as in Ⅱ.1 "In Chinese Pasta Museum, you can see the material objects and pictures of various pastas made by wheat and rice and feel the special customs and etiquette to have a better understanding of its real essence and profound culture values."

This is a very typical example of C-E translation of the introduction of tourist spots which are characterized by poetic style of excessive descriptions, parallel structures and glittering expressions.

Example 2

ST：金佛山又名金山,古称九递山,位于南川市城东40千米处,系大娄山脉东段支脉的突异山峰,绝顶海拔2 251米,占地260平方千米。在它的脚下,大溪河逶蛇而入乌江。金佛山那气势雄伟的崇山峻岭,妖娆挺拔的奇峰异石,古怪离奇的溶岩洞穴,匹练垂空的飞泉瀑布,变化万千的雾湖云海,满山清翠的茂林修竹,千姿百态的奇花异草,是名闻中外的巴蜀四大胜景,重现于这座国家级森林公园。改革开放这把时代的钥匙,打开了金佛山神秘的大门,人们惊呼它是"养在深闺人未识"的风景明珠,1988年被国务院批准为"全国重点风景名胜区",1994年又被批准为"国家级森林公园金佛山"。金佛山峭千丈,奇峰突兀,溶洞深邃,108座隽峰秀岭,座座争妍斗巧,比如香炉山、石人山、猴儿山,听听名儿就使人心痒痒地想去看看。

TT：Jinfoshan, also known as Jinshan, is located 40 kilometers east of Nanchuan City with an area of 260 square kilometers. It is the Eastern Branch of Dalou Mountain Range with the top altitude of 2,251 meters. At its foot, Daxi River meanders into Wujiang River. As one of the four most well-known scenic spots in Sichuan Province, the forest park attracts visitors by its majestic mountains, enchanting peaks and rocks, strange karst caves, flying springs and waterfalls, changing fog lakes and clouds, lush forests and bamboos, and various exotic flowers and plants. After reform and opening up, the mysterious spot appears in people's vision. It was approved as a "national key scenic spot" for its beautiful peaks and deep karst caves. Altogether, there are 108 steep and abrupt peaks and mountains with different shapes such as incense burner peak, stone-man peak and monkey peak, which can trigger people's desires to visit it.

Analysis: In the translation process, paraphrasing, omission, restructuring methods are combined to translate the text. "金佛山那气势雄伟的崇山峻岭,妖娆挺拔的奇峰异石,古怪离奇的溶岩洞穴,匹练垂空的飞泉瀑布,变化万千的雾湖云海,满山清翠的茂林修竹,千姿百态的奇花异草,是名闻中外的巴蜀四大胜景,重现于这座国家级森林公园。" are paraphrased by using different adjectives in accordance with the English norms. And the sentence structure is reorganized to make the TT idiomatic and readable. "养在深闺人未识" and "1994年又被批准为'国家级森林公园金佛山'" are omitted and compressed to avoid repetition.

Example 3

ST：泰山古称岱山,又称岱宗,位于山东省中部,为中国五岳(泰山、华山、衡山、嵩山、恒山)之一。因地处东部,故称东岳。泰山总面积426平方千米,主峰玉皇顶海拔1 532.8米,山

Chapter Three Translation of Tourism Promotional Texts

势雄伟壮丽,气势磅礴,名胜古迹众多,有"五岳独尊"之誉。孔子有"登泰山而小天下"之语。唐大诗人杜甫有"会当凌绝顶,一览众山小"的佳句。泰山在人们的心目中,已成为伟大、崇高的象征。

TT: Mount Tai was called Daishan in ancient times, also known as Daizong. Located in the middle of Shandong Province, it is one of the five most famous mountains in China. Mount Tai covers a total area of 426 square kilometers. The main peak, Yuhuangding, is 1,532.8 meters above sea level. It has many majestic, magnificent scenic spots and historic sites. It is the most exclusive among the five famous mountains because all mountains look small on the top of it. Mount Tai has become a symbol of greatness and nobility in people's minds.

Analysis: Translation methods adopted in the above example are omission, paraphrasing and restructuring. In the TT, "五岳:泰山、华山、衡山、嵩山、恒山" is omitted because foreign readers have no ideas of the name of these mountains, so it is generalized as "the five most famous mountains". The quotation "孔子有'登泰山而小天下'之语" is also deleted because it has the same meaning as Dufu's poem. The quotation "唐大诗人杜甫有'会当凌绝顶,一览众山小'的佳句" is paraphrased because it proves the magnificence of the mountain. Besides, the topic predominant structure is reconstructed into subject-predicate structure.

Example 4

ST: 华山以其峻峭吸引了无数游人。山上的观、院、亭、阁皆依山势而建,一山飞峙,恰似空中楼阁,而且有古松相映,更是别具一格。山峰秀丽,又形象各异,如似韩湘子赶牛、金蟾戏龟、白蛇遭难。

TT: Huashan Mountain attracts countless tourists because of its precipitousness. You can see the Taosism temples, countyards and pavilions along the mountain which seems fly like a castle in the air with ancient pines around, making it a unique scenery. You can imagine different images triggered by the beautiful peaks with various forms.

Analysis: Translation methods adopted in the above example include the omission of "如似韩湘子赶牛、金蟾戏龟、白蛇遭难", however, together with the sentences preceding it, it is paraphrased as "You can imagine different images triggered by the beautiful peaks with various forms". Furthermore, the second person pronoun "you" is added to make the text conform to the English style.

In summary, instead of the traditional bottom-up retrospective approach which focuses on the translation of micro-linguistic elements, translators should adopt a macro-top-down prospective approach, focusing first on the main purpose of the translation, that is, to "convert readers to tourists". The purpose of the translation is not to find linguistic equivalence for the source text in the target language, but to use the source text as a basis to create an appealing image of the tourism destination for a new audience. This purpose should serve as the guide and remain a key driver throughout the translation process. Therefore, what does not serve "the purpose" in the target language and culture, even though present in the source text, should be avoided altogether.

3.7 E-C Translation of TPTs under the Guidance of Functional Approach

As is discussed above, there are many discrepancies between English and Chinese TPTs. In order to make the TT acceptable to the TT readers, translators should make some adjustment in the translation process.

3.7.1 Translating the English plain style into Chinese poetic style

English TPTs incline to emphasize the information and effect rather than superficial language. They do not use as much superfluous description as Chinese do. Instead, they prefer plain and concise language, but this is not in line with the Chinese habits. Therefore, the plain style is often converted into Chinese poetic expression, because creating the appropriate style can determine the smooth transfer of the persuasive function.

Example 1

ST: On the road leading to Central Europe to Adriatic coast lies a small Slovenian town of Postoyna. Its subterranean world holds some of Europe's most magnificent underground galleries. Time loses all meanings in the formation of these underground wonders. Dripstones, stalactites, in different shapes—columns, pillars and translucent curtains, conjure up unforgettable images.

TT: 从中东通往亚得里亚海的路上,有一座斯洛文尼亚小城叫作博斯托伊那。这座小城的地下藏着欧洲最宏伟的地下画廊。这些地下奇观的形成使时光失去了一切意义。滴水石、钟乳石,形态各异——如梁,似柱,像透明的珠帘,如同魔法变出来的一样,令人难忘。

Example 2

ST: The harbor looked most beautiful in its semi-circle of hills and half-lights. The color of a pearl gray and a fairy texture… This Arctic scenery has a beauty which is the exact antithesis of the Christmas card of tradition. Soft, melting halftones. Nothing brittle of garish.

TT: 只见海港环抱于半圆形小山丛中,煞是好看,朦朦胧胧,一片银灰,宛若仙境……北极地区景色优美,同传统的圣诞卡适成对照。它浓淡交融,光影柔和,清雅绝俗。

Example 3

ST: For me this landscape was always a magical prospect, the austere countryside stretching away with the sharp definition of an 18th-century aquatint across hill and woodland to Mt. Battie outlined against the horizon.

TT: 我总觉得这儿的风光格外迷人,那乡间淳古浑朴的原野绵延伸展,跨过小山,越过森林,一路延伸到遥远地平线上赫然矗立的巴蒂山——好一幅轮廓鲜明的十八世纪铜板风景画!

Example 4

ST: Towers, domes, balanced rocks, and arches have been formed over millions of years of weathering and erosion, and the process continues, constantly reshaping this fantastic rock garden.

TT：岁月沧桑，风化雨蚀，造就了这里奇特的山体风貌：满山"巨塔"高耸，"穹丘"浑圆，"不倒翁"摇摇欲坠，"大拱门"凌空而立，奇形怪状，浑然天成。大自然的鬼斧神工创造了这神奇美丽的石头公园。

Example 5

ST：Tiny islands are strung around the edge of the peninsula like a pearl necklace. Hunks of coral reef, coconut palms, and fine white sand.

TT：座座岛屿玲珑小巧，紧密相连，像一串串珍珠缀成的项链，环绕着半岛边缘。岛上珊瑚礁红，椰树成片，沙滩如银，景色如诗如画。

By comparing TT with ST, we can see that different translation methods such as paraphrasing, restructuring and amplification are adopted in the above examples. Furthermore, all English subject-predicate sentences are transformed into paratactic Chinese topic predominant sentences.

3.7.2　Translating English adjectives or other descriptive words into Chinese four-character phrases (*Chengyu*)

Example 1

ST：A fascinating city between sea and sky, like Venus rising from the waves, Venus welcomes tourists from the five continents drawn to her by the charm of her water and pellucid light, free from all dust and cooled by the sea breeze. She also offers the intellectual pleasures to be derived from her masterpieces which mark the meeting of East and West.

TT：威尼斯水城海天相连，景色迷人，宛如碧波中踏浪而来的维纳斯，吸引着五大洲的游客。她水色旖旎，波光澄澈，清风拂面而来，褪去你心中的不快与烦恼。而城中那些集东西方艺术之大成的艺术杰作，更给人以精神上的享受。

Example 2

ST：The Glacier Express cuts a cross-section through stunning Switzerland—pure train-travel pleasure. Prepare to be pampered in the Glacier Express. Savour meals specially prepared by our chef served in our stylish dining car. Or relax in your comfortable seat and enjoy coffee, snacks and drinks served from our minibar. The Glacier-Express is superb in all four seasons：shimmering peaks in summer, snow-covered, fairy-tale scenery in winter, fabulous Alpine flowers in spring and a kaleidoscope of color in autumn.

TT：冰川快车横穿魅力无穷的瑞士，让您尽享火车旅行的乐趣。轻松舒适地坐在座位上享受厨师为您精心烹制的风味美食，或品尝迷你酒吧为您精心准备的香浓咖啡、各色小吃和饮料。一年四季，冰川快车都带给您无与伦比的旅行体验。春季，阿尔卑斯山鲜花怒放；夏季，群峰在阳光下熠熠生辉；秋季，各种色彩缤纷绚烂；冬季，整个世界如童话世界般粉妆玉砌。

3.7.3　Transforming the second person pronoun to the third person pronoun

English TPTs exploit first-person and second-person pronouns such as "you", "we", "your" and "our" to create a friendship-like relationship between the host and the potential tourist. However, Chinese writers usually use "the visitor" or zero pronoun to address the reader with a formal tone. Therefore, in translation, adjustment from the second person to the third person (or omitting personal pronoun) must be made to adapt to the TT culture. Example:

ST: In the afternoon, <u>you</u> can explore the city by bicycle—and the fact that bikes for both adults and children can be rented for free makes this method of transportation more fun. Bikes are available all year round from Velogate by the Swiss National Museum and, from May to October, from outside Globs, the opera House and Swissotel Oerlikon.

TT:下午可以骑自行车游览整个城市。免费租用适合成人及儿童的自行车,会给旅行增加更多的乐趣。瑞士国家博物馆附近的福乐门(Velogate)全年提供自行车租赁服务。五月至十月期间,<u>游客</u>还能在格劳博城、歌剧院及欧瑞康瑞士酒店外租到自行车。

Analysis: In the above example, "you" in the first sentence is omitted, but in the last sentence, the implied second person pronoun is explicitly translated as "游客", because this can make the sentence coherent with the preceding sentences.

3.7.4　Translating English TPTs as a whole

Generally speaking, the TPTs as a whole are more complicated than the above examples, so a comprehensive method is adopted to make the TT acceptable.

Example 1

ST:　　　　　　　　　Washington Cathedral

The Washington Cathedral was constructed by traditional methods used by <u>craftspeople</u> from Europe over the centuries. It is gothic in design and the details of its construction are <u>readily available</u> at the Cathedral. It is a functioning church, with several chapels below the main level. The stained glass windows are <u>unique</u> and each tells a story. The grounds of the cathedral are <u>well maintained</u> and there are many quiet spots for <u>contemplation and enjoyment of the view</u> as the highest point in the District of Columbia. The Cathedral gift shop and the Herb Cottage Gift shop are well worth a visit.

TT:　　　　　　　　　华盛顿大教堂

华盛顿大教堂是几个世纪以来欧洲的<u>能工巧匠</u>采用传统技法建造而成的,其哥特式的设计在大教堂的每个建筑细节都<u>随处可见</u>。这是一座正常运转的教堂,在主层下方有几个小教堂。彩色玻璃窗<u>别具一格</u>,每一扇似乎都在讲述一个故事。大教堂的地面<u>平整光滑</u>,作为哥伦比亚特区的至高点,有许多安静的地方可供人们<u>沉思默想、欣赏美景</u>。大教堂的礼品店和赫伯小屋礼品店同样值得驻足游览。

Example 2

ST:　　　　　　　　　Las Vegas Recommended Tours

Las Vegas may be known as the "sin city", but it has a lot of great attractions. Certainly, the casinos and nightlife are what bring visitors here, but there are so much more to do. There are several historic and interesting sites that are perfect for guided or self-guided tours.

Chapter Three　Translation of Tourism Promotional Texts

The Hoover Dam is one of Nevada's proudest possessions. It displaces the Colorado River and creates Lake Mead, a large man-made waterway. You'll find a delicious meal at one of the many restaurants found within the Lake Mead National Recreation Area. At night, try the Lake Mead Cruise for dinner and dancing as well as beautiful scenery. There is even a nearby theater, the Regal Boulder Station that shows contemporary films.

TT：　　　　　　　　　　拉斯维加斯推荐旅游

拉斯维加斯也许被称为"罪恶之城",但它却有很多引人入胜之处。当然,赌场和夜生活是吸引游客的主要原因,但绝非仅此而已。这里的历史名胜和有趣景点非常适合导游或自助旅游。

胡佛大坝是内华达州最值得骄傲的景点之一。大坝围起的米德湖取代了科罗拉多河,形成了一条宽阔的人工水道。在米德湖国家娱乐区内,餐厅云集,美食随处可觅。晚上,游客可以踏上米德湖游轮,观赏美景,享受晚餐,尽情欢舞。如果想看电影,在附近的影院和帝王博尔德车站均可观看到最流行的影片。

Example 3

ST：　　　　　　　　　　The Maasai Mara

The Maasai Mara is one of the best-known reserves in the whole of Africa, and is globally renowned for its exceptional wildlife. Despite comprising only 0.01% of Africa's total landmass, more than 40% of Africa's larger mammals can be found here. Across the vast plains of the Mara, visitors are able to witness lions, cheetahs, leopards, elephants, and an infinite variety of other species in their natural habitats.

The Maasai Mara lies in the Great Rift Valley, which is a fault line some 3,500 miles (5,600 km) long stretching from Ethiopia's Red Sea through Kenya, Tanzania, Malawi, and into Mozambique. Here the valley is wide, and a towering escarpment can be seen in the hazy distance. The animals are at liberty to move outside the park into huge areas known as "dispersal areas". There can be as much wildlife roaming outside the park as inside. Many Maasai villages are located in the "dispersal areas" and they have, over centuries, developed a synergetic relationship with the wildlife.

Mara and Serengeti parks are interdependent wildlife havens. This is where the world's largest multi-species migration takes place. The movement is, centered around the wildebeest migrating from Serengeti into Masai Maara during the dry period in Tanzania, crossing the mighty Mara River on their way.

TT：　　　　　　　　　　马赛马拉

马赛马拉是整个非洲最著名的保护区之一,以其独特的野生动物闻名于世。尽管只占非洲陆地总面积的0.01%,但在这里可以找到40%以上的非洲大型哺乳动物。在马拉广阔的平原上,游客可以看到狮子、猎豹、豹子、大象以及各种各样的其他物种在这里栖息繁衍。

马赛马拉河位于东非大裂谷。这是一条从埃塞俄比亚红海经肯尼亚、坦桑尼亚、马拉维延伸至莫桑比克约3 500英里(5 600千米)长的断层带。这里山谷宽阔,朦胧远处悬崖高耸。公园内外,野生动物成群结队,自由撒欢。许多马赛村庄也处于"分散区",几个世纪以来,它们与野生动物和谐相处。

马拉公园和塞伦盖蒂公园是相互依存的野生动物庇护所。每年,这里是世界上最大的多物种迁徙地。在坦桑尼亚的旱季,以角马为主的大迁徙,从塞伦盖蒂出发,经过马赛马拉,一路穿过浩瀚无边的马拉河,绝尘而去。

Analysis: The above translations read smooth and idiomatic to Chinese readers because several translation methods such as paraphrasing, restructuring are adopted together to make the TT acceptable.

In short, the criterion for tourism translation is not whether the version is faithful to the original text, but whether it achieves the intended functions of arousing the target reader's interest and offering tourist information clearly and accurately. In order to achieve this goal, the translator should not employ word-for-word translation and rigidly adhere to the form. Instead, he/she should decide what kind of information to include in the messages to ensure maximum impact in culturally different settings so that he/she can create a text based on the given information. Furthermore, the translator should try to cater to the target reader's aesthetic taste and make the translation a strong appeal to the reader with the most appropriate translation strategies.

Chapter Four Translation of News Report

4.1 Relevant Concepts of News Report

4.1.1 Definition of News

News is the information people read, hear and watch every day that explains what is happening around them. The abbreviation NEWS stands for "Notable Events, Weather and Sports". The *Oxford English Dictionary* defines news as "tidings; the report or account of recent events or occurrences, brought or coming to one as new information". According to Keeble (1998:159), news is a report of an event containing timely (or at least unknown) information, which has been accurately gathered and written by trained reporters for the purpose of serving the reader, listener or viewer.

In China, the generally recognized influential definition is the one given by Lu Dingyi (Xu, 2003: 4). In 1943, Lu wrote in his article "Our Basic Concept of Journalism": "News is a report of the fact that has recently happened." The press circle unanimously agrees that this definition is both concise and clear, and discloses the features of news. Firstly, as compared with other text types, the content of news is "fact"; secondly, as compared with history, the "fact" happened "recently"; thirdly, "fact" is just a source of news but not news itself, unless it is "reported".

Whatever the definition may be, news is characterized by being objective, timely and public. Besides, news comes from society and it is reported to meet the needs of the public—the people living in the society.

We are now living in an information era with many channels such as TV, newspapers and Internet to get news. News reports transmit information about economics, politics, culture, sports, music and art, etc. at an unprecedented speed, which facilitates contact and understanding between people all over the world.

For Chinese people, English news is the most direct, effective and convenient way to understand world affairs. Therefore, translation of English news plays an increasingly important role in our daily life and work.

4.1.2 Structure of News Report

News report, as a special type of text, has its unique structure. It is made up of three parts. Namely, headline, lead and body.

Of the three elements, the headline is the soul of a news item because it conveys the main idea of the news. By only reading the headline of an article, the readers can immediately learn what the story is about. It is always eye-catching with large print and sometimes written with language of sensational effect to attract the inquisitive readers' attention and lead them into the story.

News lead is the opening sentence or paragraph of the news, which serves as a brief introduction. As the name indicates, it "leads" to the rest part of the story. News lead often contains the information that the readers are eager to know such as the five Ws+H —*who*, *what*, *when*, *where and why*, and *how*, the sixth element. The freelance writer Robert M. Knight once said: "For a journalist, it is imperative to get the audience's and the editor's attention with the least amount of writing… Regardless of what kind of writing is involved, the principle is the same. The first words, the first phrases, the first paragraphs are critical." Thus the lead must arouse the readers' interest and curiosity and lure them to read the whole story.

The rest of a news story is called the body, which is a further development of the lead with details of the facts. The body is the biggest part of a news reporting, which is often organized in the following three ways: inverted pyramid structure, pyramid structure and mixed structure. The inverted pyramid structure refers to the way to present facts in the order of descending importance and this arrangement can inform the readers with the most important information first. It is, in fact, the most frequently used form in news reports. The pyramid structure, also called the chronological structure, presents the facts in a natural and chronological order and this arrangement can make the readers follow the logical development of the story easily and improve the readers' suspense and interest. The mixed structure, which is a mix of the previous structures, often begins with a summary lead which always introduces the outline of the event, followed by the paragraphs reporting the whole event chronologically. This form can leave readers an impression of complete content and clear narration.

4.2 Characteristics of News Language

4.2.1 Stylistic characteristics of news language

Martin Joos (1962) in his *The Five Clocks* classified language style into five types—the frozen style/the rigid style, the formal style, the consultative style, the casual style, and the intimate style. The former two types are grouped as "the formal style" and the latter ones are of "the informal style".

Formal English, also known as "King's English", pursues strict and precise expressive rules and applies to formal and solemn writings. Neutral/Standard English is popularly used by educated users, which conforms to the fixed expressive rules but allows moderate changes. Informal English/colloquialism, derived from oral language, have greater freedom in structure and word usage.

Language used in English news belongs to general English, a type of Standard English or Neutral English. However since the 1960s, a great amount of colloquial words and slang have found their way into English news due to the rapid growth of modern mass media. As Newmark has grouped news into informative text type, news language is destined to be "modern, non-regional, non-class and non-dialectal", since the core of the informative function of language is "external situation, the facts of topic, reality outside language, including reported ideas or theories." (Newmark, 88: 40)

The language of news reports in both English and Chinese share many similarities. Both not only follow the accepted rules of grammar and sentence patterns, but also carry certain special features such as brevity, concreteness, accuracy, popularity and vividness (Xu, 2003: 21).

1. Brevity

Generally speaking, news is supposed to be brief in content and concise in language since the space or room of the media is always limited. Redundancy in language is highly inappropriate in news writing. Superfluous words and unnecessary sentences should be avoided and priority should be given to short, simple and perspicuous sentences over long, complex and obscure ones.

2. Concreteness

The specific statement of the six elements in news report—*when*, *where*, *who*, *what*, *why* and *how*, describe the details of a news event, so the narration of events, description of scenes, delineation of characters and behaviors call for concrete words and concrete expressions which can reflect the authenticity and credibility of the news.

3. Accuracy

Accuracy is the core of news language. Since the main purpose of news reports is to present the news event in an objective, true and precise manner, it has to be communicated by accurate expression. Inaccurate language will hinder the readers from obtaining the truth of the events, so reporters should give priority to word choice in writing.

4. Popularity

News is closely related to the media and the intended addressee of news is the general public. Readers of newspapers and audiences of radio and television are from all walks of life, different vocational and educational background and different age groups. In order to meet their needs, news language should be popular and accessible.

5. Vividness

Vividness is the typical feature of news language. In order to achieve the vivid and intriguing effect, many grammatical alterations and rhetorical devices are employed in news reports. The vividness of news language can be best reflected in headlines.

6. Objectivity

News language must be fair. Words which may lead to biased view of people, events or situation should be avoided. In order to be safe, journalists usually are very careful in choosing adjectives and adverbs in news language, especially when describing disputes or conflicts.

4.2.2 Lexical characteristics of news language

1. Preference for short words—midget words

The excessive use of short words, such as monosyllabic words or disyllabic words, is one of the most distinguishing features of English news language. News reporters or writers tend to prefer short words to longer ones due to one journalistic principle "Saying a lot in least space." (Mencher, 1994: 102). For example,

Bhutto's husband calls for UN *probe* (*investigation*)
Quake death toll may *top* 2000 (*exceed*)
New groups *boost* Hi-tech research (*promote*)
Baker, Japan Visit Off, *Arms* Issue Hot. (*The Military Weapons*)
Minister seeks *nod* for oil saving plan. (*approval*)
Bug kills babies (*disease*)
New *stance* to power cuts (*attitude*)
Bank rate *cut* (*reduction*)

The following are more short nouns often seen in news reports, which can be used to replace the latter word.

aid = assistance	blast = explosion	cop = policeman
drive = campaign	envoy = ambassador	feud = dispute
nod = approval	output = production	talk = conference
probe = investigation	rift = separation	stance = attitude

Besides nouns, short verbs are also preferred to longer ones in news reports. For examples,

ease = lessen/relieve	end = terminate	flay = criticize
flout = insult	foil = prevent from	gut = destroy
head = direct	hold = arrest	laud = praise
mark = celebrate	name = nominate	moot = discuss
mull = consider	nab = arrest	nip = defeat
slay = murder	soar = skyrocket	spur = encourage

swap=exchange	*loom = happen*	*mar=damage*
ace=champion	*body=committee*	*clash=controversy*
crash=collision	*deal=agreement*	*dems=democrats*
fake=counterfeit	*fete=celebration*	*flop=failure*
freeze=stabilization	*glut=oversupply*	*pact= treaty*
poll=election	*pullout=withdrawal*	*row=quarrel*
set=ready	*step=progress*	*strife=conflict*
ties=(diplomatic) relations	*snag=unexpected difficulty*	*nab=arrest*
axe=dismiss	*ban = prohibit*	*blast =explode*
boost= improve	*cut = reduce*	*hit=strike*
eye=witness	*attack = criticize*	*quit= resign*
apt=choose	*shift =transfer*	*top=exceed*

2. Preference for new words—neologism

In *Longman Advanced American Dictionary*, neologism is defined as "a new word or expression, or a word used with a new meaning" (Longman, 2003: 973). In our life, new discoveries, inventions and technological equipment are being made every day; new ideas, thoughts and new social fashions are emerging one after another. When reporting these new events and phenomena, journalists sometimes have to coin names for them. Accordingly, a large number of new words appear. For example, with the development of science and technology, new words such as online education（在线教学）, autotune（电音修饰人声）, infomercial（商业信息电视片）, cyberian（网络用户）, biotech（生物科技）, vape（吸电子烟）, view data（图像数据）, video conference（可视电话会议）, spyware（间谍软件）, mouse potato（网虫）, cyber squatter（网络蟑螂）, Internetese（网络语言）, bio-chips（生物芯片）, technofreak（科技迷）appear as a result.

Neologism reflecting new social phenomena is often created by journalists as well. For example, computernik（电脑迷）, Phubber（低头族）, online celebrity（网红）, click in（打卡）, hard core（硬核）, group purchase（团购）, E-commerce livestreaming（电商直播）, laundering（洗钱）, bioterrorism（生物恐怖主义）, folknik（民族迷）, jobnik（工作狂）, kickback（回扣）are newly invented words often seen in news reports.

In most cases, these new words first appear in news reports and soon spread through mass media and become popular. For example:

Chinese Spring Festival PK Western Christmas

In this example, the new word "PK" originates from "player-killing", a word from popular computer games. It is now commonly used in entertainment reports with the meaning of "competing". In Chinese news reports, we can also find many new words, which frequently appear in different kinds of media. For examples:

给力 gelivable	偷菜 vegeteal	胶囊公寓 capsule apartment
蜗居 tiny house	团购 group purchase	伪娘 cross-dresser
秒杀 seckilling	裸捐 all-out donation	围观 circusee

网红 online celebrity　　网剧 webisode　　炫富 flaunt wealth
翻拍 reshoot　　　　　　招牌菜 signature dishes　　托儿 salesperson's decoy
恶搞 spoof　　　　　　　晕菜 numbed, dumbfounded　跑酷 parkour
大腕 top notch　　　　　搬迁户 relocated families　　假唱 lip-synch

3. Wide use of abbreviations and acronyms

In order to save space, abbreviations and acronyms are frequently used in newspaper headlines. Abbreviations or shortened words are the clippings which keep the first part, the middle part or the ending part of the original words, while the rest parts are shortened or clipped away for the sake of saving space. Acronyms or initials are formed by the first letters of a phrase or proper names and printed in capitalized letters. The following are some examples.

Abbreviations

flu—influenza　　　　　　fridge—refrigerator　　　amt.—amount
con—convict　　　　　　　deli—delicatessen　　　　pct—percent
apt—apartment　　　　　　acctg—accounting　　　　affl—affiliation
alt—alter　　　　　　　　almn—alumni　　　　　　bud—budget
eq—equivalent　　　　　　err—error　　　　　　　excp—exception
app.—appendix　　　　　　approx.—approximately　　ave.—avenue
Bio—biology　　　　　　　capt.—captain　　　　　　cent.—centigrade
univ.—university　　　　　sq.—square　　　　　　　fcn—function
entr—enter　　　　　　　govt—government　　　　int'l—international
tech—technology　　　　　hosp—hospital　　　　　　expo—exposition
maint—maintenance　　　　max—maximum　　　　　msg—message
mtd—Month-to-Date　　　　nbr—number　　　　　　opr—operator
biz—business　　　　　　champ—champion　　　　dorm—dormitory

Initials

CBD—Central Business District
IMF—International Monetary Fund
IOC—International Olympic Committee
UNCF—United Nations Children's Fund
UNESCO—United Nations Educational, Scientific, and Cultural Organization
UNPKF—United Nations Peace-Keeping Force
WWF—World Wildlife Fund
DJI—Dow-Jones Index
PT—Public Relations
SDI—Strategic Defence Initiative
PM—Prime Minister
GM—General Manager

VIP—*Very Important Person*
NPU—*Northwestern Polytechnical University*
WHO—*World Health Organization*
WTO—*World Trade Organization*

4.2.3 Syntactic characteristics of news language

Syntax is concerned with the rules for ordering and connecting words into sentences, which allow various possibilities to be exploited for effective linguistic communication. Stories fall apart without logically conceived paragraphs. Paragraphs deteriorate without solid, readable sentences (Mencher, 1987: 97). Thus the foundation of a good writing is to create sentences that are so well-organized and so expressive that readers can read easily from the first word of a news story to the end. That is to say, sentences play an important role in realizing the fundamental function of news report.

To understand how news function is created through sentences, we should focus not only on the basic aspects such as sentence structure, voice and tense but also the features of its own in comparison with sentences in other texts.

1. Frequent use of expanded simple sentences

With regard to simple sentences, it ought to be observed first that there are degrees in simplicity. A simple sentence contains only one main clause and no subordinate clauses, but it may contain a compound subject or a compound predicate or both. The subject and the predicate can be expanded with adjectives, adverbs, prepositional phrases, appositives, and verbal phrases. In this way, an expanded simple sentence can carry with it much more information in a still simple and clear sentence structure.

As a news report is written to attract the most possible readers, it must be easily understood by people of different education backgrounds. Therefore, simple sentence structures are preferred and often adopted by journalists because they can show a clear logical relationship of information to readers and make it easier for readers to understand. Robert Gunning, a former consultant who studied more than 100 daily newspapers, wrote "I know of no author addressing a general audience today with an average of more than 20 words per sentence and still succeeds in getting published" (Mencher, 1994: 32). Under such circumstance, expanded simple sentences suit best in news reporting writing. For example:

The Youth Olympic Games (YOG) are an elite sporting event for young people from all over the world. But an event distinct from other youth sports competitions, as they also include a series of educational activities with three areas of focus: protecting the athletes, working on performance, and assisting the athletes outside sport.

The sports programme is mainly based on that of the Olympic Games. In addition, it includes exciting new sports, disciplines and formats, such as breaking, sport climbing, 3×3 basketball, 3×3 ice hockey and mixed gender and mixed National Olympic Committee (NOC) events.

Away from the field of play, the education programme uses a variety of fun and interactive activities, workshops and team-building exercises to give the participating athletes the opportunity to learn about the Olympic values, explore other cultures, develop the skills to become true ambassadors of their sport, and improve their training methods and performance.

The Youth Olympic Games are aimed at bringing together talented young athletes aged from 15 to 18 from around the world.

The most recent Summer YOG in Buenos Aires in 2018 featured 4,000 athletes and achieved gender equality for the first time. The latest Winter YOG took place in Lausanne in 2020 and featured 1,872 athletes.

(https://olympics.com/ioc/youth-olympic-games)

As the example shows, to maximize the effect of transmitting the latest information, the journalist put as much information as possible in one simple sentence to help the readers to get much information in the shortest possible time with the greatest ease.

However, it is inappropriate to say that news reports use only short simple sentences. Aesthetics of news writing require all kinds of sentences to be used. It is often neither economical nor rhythmic for news writers to put forward an idea by using one simple sentence after another. In fact, a complex sentence that can state relations more precisely and more economically than a string of simple sentences or compound sentences joined by "and", "but", "so", etc. As the sentence becomes longer, it will provide more information to help the readers to understand the news orassociate something related to the news. For example:

1) *An extremely powerful Hurricane Laura has ripped apart portions of Louisiana and far-eastern Texas, killing at least three people and tearing up roofs while knocking out power for hundreds of thousands after first roaring ashore as a Category 4 storm.*

(CNN, Aug. 27, 2020)

2) *Rivera, who was confirmed dead at age 33 after her body was found on July 13, days after she had tragically gone missing during a boating trip at Lake Piru with her son, starred alongside Riley on the hit musical television series Glee.*

(Yahoo, Aug. 28, 2020)

Generally speaking, the journalists tend to use more expanded simple sentences mixed with some complicated sentences.

2. Voice—active voice plus passive voice

Like other English writing, both active voice and passive voice are used in News writing. Active voice is more direct and vigorous as said by Gunning: "Strong-flavored, active verbs give writing bounce and hold reader's attention" (Mencher,1994:35). It tells the reader who is doing an action, and makes sentences move at a swift pace, thus creating the effects of directness and straightforwardness. As a result, active voice is preferred in journalistic English. However, passive voice still has its place. It is used when the recipient of an action is the most important element in the news (such as disaster, the injured in accidents, and the victims in crimes) or when it is unnecessity to mention the "doer" of an action. For example:

1) *Famous singer Lady Gaga announced on April 6 that she had curated an online charity concert named "One World: Together at Home" in collaboration with the WHO. The concert <u>will be televised</u> and <u>streamed</u> globally on April 18 and the funds raised from the concert <u>will be used</u> to support medical workers on the COVID-19 front line. The starry lineup of the event includes Elton John, pianist Lang Lang, Billie Ellish, etc.*

(chinadaily.cn, Apr. 16, 2020)

2) *An eight-month-old female panda cub died due to accidental suffocation in Wolong National Nature Reserve, Sichuan Province. The panda was found dead by a breeder on April 9 with ropes of a hanging ball tangled around its neck and forelegs, which <u>was speculated</u> to be the cause of the suffocation.*

(chinadaily.cn, Apr. 16, 2020)

In the above examples, active voice and passive voice are used together to transmit the information more accurately and appropriately. Since passive voice is not frequently used in Chinese, it should be dealt flexibly in E-C translation.

3. Frequent use of both direct and indirect speech

To make the news sound true and vivid, direct speeches are frequently used in news reports. It indicates that the news report is objective and free from journalist's personal viewpoint. For example:

1) *Hours after Raducanu had won the championship, she found time to send a message to her fans in China in fluent Mandarin. "Hi, everyone," she said in the video posting. "I want to say thank you to you guys and I hope you could enjoy my tennis. I'm thrilled to win. Love you all." Raducanu's mother Renee—full name Dong Mei zhai grew up in Shenyang, a city in north-east China. Overnight, the number of Raducanu's followers on Instagram more than doubled to 1.3 m.*

(chinadaily.cn, Sep. 16, 2021)

2) *However, Chinese Foreign Ministry spokesman Hong Lei told a news briefing: "Blaming these misdeeds on China is unacceptable. Hacking is an international problem and China is also a victim. The claims of so-called support for hacking are completely unfounded and have ulterior motives."*

(BBC, Jun. 2, 2019)

Quotations are often introduced by the following words: *say, tell, add, repeat, state, go on, repeat, point out, proclaim, explain, report, elaborate, reaffirm, reiterate, call, declare, proclaim, claim, allege, comment, observe, note, stress, emphasize, reply, answer, insist, urge, reveal, disclose, assert, admit, concede, confess, deny, renounce, promise, analyze, warn, contend, maintain, object, suggest, challenge, refute, argue, propose, protest, complain,* etc. Among these words, "say" is used most frequently.

What's more, the position of the introductory words is flexible in news. For example:

1) *Trump on Twitter called* his brief discussions with House Speaker Nancy Pelosi and Senate Democratic leader Chuck Schumer "a total waste of time."

(chinadaily. cn, Sep. 20, 2019)

2) Both were African Americans, <u>said Leesburge police spokeman Chris Jones</u>, and both remain hospitalized. A third man, a dark-skinned Latino, was attacked in a shopping-center parking lot in Leesburge on Friday, but this time with a hammer, <u>Jones said</u>.

(Seatle Times, Aug. 10, 2010)

4.3 Criteria and Principles for News Report Translation

4.3.1 Functionalist criteria for the translation of news report

Generally speaking, translation standards are universal for all kinds of texts. The translation of news is one of the branches of translation, therefore the general translation criterion is also fit for the translation of news. However, because of the distinguished features of news language, the criterion of news translation has its special characteristics.

1. Accuracy

Since news reports cover social, political, financial, military, scientific, technological as well as cultural field of the society, there is a large scale of diction in news language. As a result, the correctness of translation mainly lies on the translation of technical terms and new words. Take the word "recorder" for example. Its original meaning is tape-recorder or a person who keeps a record of events or facts, but when it is used in a piece of news about contentious case, it turns into a typical legal technical term, which refers to a judge（法官）in a court of law in some parts of Britain and the US. If it is translated as "记录官" or "录音机" according to its literal meaning, it would be inaccurate. Another case in point is the word "labor". When it is used in medical or health news, it refers to the period of time or the process of giving birth to a baby rather than physical work.

2. Readability

Since news often bears a strong nature of popularity, the language in the version should be easy, interesting and enjoyable to meet the taste of readers in all walks of life.

3. Appropriateness

Because of the great variety of news types, the style of news should also be taken into consideration in translation. Therefore, translators should employ different methods to translate different news, and the style adopted should be in harmony with the original one. For example, as far as the translation of political news is concerned, serious and formal language should be used.

4. Timeliness

News is used to report the events that are happening in the rapidly changing world, so it must be reported timely. Otherwise, the news will become outdated and obsolete.

5. Vividness

In order to make the language vivid and eye-catching, journalists often employ rhetorical devices such as metaphor, metonymy, analogy, allusion and pun, etc. to attract readers. In addition, new words are also used to create the effect of popularity. Therefore, translators should take effective measures to convey the vividness to the target readers.

It must be pointed out that there are no rigid criteria in translation. The translator should apply different criteria in accordance with different text types, the features of the times, social and cultural elements and so on.

4.3.2 Functionalist principles for the translation of news reports

1. Reader-centered principle

The functions of news text mainly lie in sending messages and attracting readers. In other words, the language used in journalism serves the informative function, the persuasive function and the aesthetic function, with the first as the primary and dominant and the latter two as the secondary and subordinate. Newmark holds that in the translation of informative and vocative types, more attention should be paid to the TT readers, and their expectations and psychological feelings to obtain the expected communication effect. Therefore, a reader-oriented approach is proved to be the main approach to the news translation.

To be specific, when a translator deals with news translation, first, he/she has to be familiar with the convention of the target language, English or Chinese. Second, he/she should know the intended function of the text and the potential readers and their expectation, the time and place for the news to release, the medium over which the news will be transmitted, and the motive for the production or reception of the news.

2. Loyalty principle

According to Nord (2001:126), loyalty refers to the interpersonal relationship between the translator, the source-texts sender, the target-text addressee and the initiator. Loyalty principle requires the translator to take account of the difference of the two cultures and helps the translator to infer and respect the communicative intention of the SL so that the translator can transmit the information faithfully to the numerous possible readers the maximum amount of intelligible information to target readers.

4.4 Translation of News Headlines

4.4.1 Characteristics of news headlines

1. Tenses in headlines

The tense of the English sentences in news writing is very flexible just like that in other kinds of writing. All tenses are used in corresponding contexts. However, the use of tense in news headlines has special features because journalists usually prefer to use brief expressions to create a sense of immediacy and catch the readers' attention immediately.

(1) Using simple present for past time or future time

English headlines under most circumstances are written in the present or future tense. The present tense emphasizes the timeliness of the news, thus giving the readers a psychologically deceptive impression that they are reading the newest stories. Besides, an effective way to abbreviate a headline is to use verbs in their present tense instead of past tense. For example:

Japan's Prime Minister Shinzo Abe resigns for health reasons
因健康原因日本首相安倍晋三辞职

(*CNN, Aug. 28, 2020*)

It is reported that Shinzo Abe, the longest-serving Japanese prime minister in history, has resigned, citing health reasons.

The headline above uses the present tense to convey to the readers a sense of immediacy for a past event, which leaves the impression among readers that the event is still happening or just happened and thus narrows the gap between readers and the news. Here is another example.

President Xi says China opposes any intervention in its internal affairs
习近平说,中国反对一切对中国内政的干涉

(*China Daily, Sept. 16, 2020*)

President Xi made the remarks when co-hosting a leaders' meeting on Sept. 14 in Beijing via video link with German Chancellor Angela Merkel. He said that Beijing would resolutely oppose any actions trying to instigate instability, division or chaos in the country. But in the headline, simple present tense is used for future events to emphasize the importance and imminence.

(2) Using present participle for occurring action

In English headlines, present participle structure is often used other than present progressive tense to save space. For example:

1) *Trial Coming to Close in Harvard Bias Lawsuit*
哈佛大学录取歧视诉讼即将完毕

(*VOA, Nov. 3, 2018*)

2) Hurricane Laura remnants *heading* toward Northeast
飓风"劳拉"残余正向东北方向移动

(ABC News, Aug. 28, 2020)

3) Freshman US Lawmakers *Setting* New Rules for Social Media
国会新科议员为社交媒体谱写新篇

(VOA, Jan. 11, 2019)

4) Bloomberg *spending* $100 million to boost Biden campaign in Florida
布隆伯格将在佛州砸下一亿美元帮助拜登竞选

(Newsy, Sept. 14, 2020)

(3) Using infinitive phrases for future time

There are many ways to express future time in English. Most headlines, however, show great favor over "be + infinitive" pattern, and even use infinitive phrases alone for future time because this makes the event sound more imminent. For instance,

1) Trump: US *to Put* Tariffs on $11B in EU Goods
特朗普：美国要对110亿美元欧盟产品加征关税

(VOA, Apr. 10, 2019)

2) Japan's Abe *to step down* as leader owing to health concerns
日本首相安倍晋三因健康问题下台

(China Daily, Aug. 28, 2020)

3) France Plans *to Crack Down* on Anti-government Protesters
法国计划严厉打击非法游行抗议活动

(VOA, Jan. 8, 2019)

In the above examples, the infinitive phrases are used to indicate future actions.

(4) Using past participle for passive voice

The passive voice in a headline puts what it tries to emphasize in foremost position and that is why the passive voice appears frequently in English news headlines. However, to use space efficiently, the auxiliary verb is often left out and the headline writers often select the past participle to indicate a passive voice. For example:

1) Legal organs *urged* to hasten reform
加快推进司法机构改革

(China Daily, Aug. 28, 2020)

2) 50,000 allowed back home as gains *made* on California wildfires
加州救火有进展，五万人回归家园

(ABC News, Aug., 2020)

3) Artificial nose *developed* to augment dogs to sniff out fentanyl
新出的人工鼻子帮助狗狗嗅出芬太尼

(VOA, Apr. 5, 2020)

4) Christmas Travelers *Snowed* Under in Europe
欧洲大雪使节日旅客受阻

(VOA, Dec. 25, 2017)

5) *Pakistan: 12 Million Affected by Devastating Floods*
巴基斯坦：洪水受灾民众达 1 200 万

(VOA, Aug. 7, 2018)

The headlines above used past participles to perform the function of passive voice.

2. Frequent omission of certain words in headlines

According to standard grammar, the headline should be a complete sentence with adequate information. But for the sake of saving space for succinctness, some grammatical parts, especially the functional words, such as the article, the conjunction "and", the verb "to be" and personal pronouns, are often omitted. The following are some examples to illustrate these omissions.

(1) Omission of articles

1) *Film industry needs at least 3 years to recover from pandemic: HK insider*
(= *The film industry needs at least 3 years to recover from pandemic: HK insider*)
电影业至少需要三年时间才能从疫情中恢复：香港内部人士报

(China Daily, Aug. 28, 2020)

2) *Christchurch killer to stay in jail until he dies*
(= *The Christchurch killer is to stay in jail until he dies*)
清真寺案凶手被判终身监禁

(BBC, Sept. 8, 2020)

(2) Omission of conjunction

1) *Hurricane Laura's rain, winds lash Louisiana*
(= *Hurricane Laura's rain and winds lash Louisiana*)
飓风"劳拉"的暴雨狂风袭击路易斯安那州

(ABC News, Aug. 28, 2020)

2) *Convicted child rapist, murderer put to death*
(= *Convicted child rapist and murderer was put to death*)
被判有罪的儿童强奸犯和杀人犯被处死

(The Washington Times, Aug. 28, 2020)

3) *China, U.S. Forces Need to co-operate*
(= *China and U.S. Forces Need to Co-operate*)
中美两军需要合作

(CNN, May 19, 2017)

(3) Omission of personal pronouns

1) *Dan Bongino, wife stalked by black lives matter activists outside RNC*
(= *Dan Bongino and his wife were stalked by black lives matter activists outside RNC*)
丹•邦吉诺和妻子在 RNC 外被黑人人权运动者跟踪

(The Washington Times, Aug. 28, 2020)

2) *EU wants to set up own defense*

(*EU wants to set up its own defense*)

欧盟希望建立自己的防御体系

(*China daily*, *Dec. 8*, *1999*)

3) *Boy*, *14*, *guilty of killing friends in ecstasy prank*

(*Boy*, *14*, *guilty of killing his friends in ecstasy prank*)

男孩,14岁,在摇头丸恶作剧中杀害朋友

(*The Times*, *May 2*, *2000*)

(4) Omission of the link verb "to be"

1) *Shenzhen to implement personal bankruptcy rule*

(= *Shenzhen is to implement personal bankruptcy rule*)

深圳将实施个人破产制

(*China Daily*, *Aug. 28*, *2020*)

2) *Severe weather possible on East Coast Saturday*

(= *Severe weather is possible on East Coast Saturday*)

东海岸周六可能出现恶劣天气

(*ABC News*, *Aug. 28*, *2020*)

From the above examples, we can see that most omitted words are functional words that do not affect the readers' understanding of the whole sentence. But sometimes, some content words, such as verb and noun, can also be omitted if the omission has fewer or almost no effect on the understanding of the whole sentence. For example:

1) *Great Wall winds through autumn mists in Hebei*

(= *Great Wall winds goes through autumn mists in Hebei*)

长城的风吹过河北的秋雾

(*China Daily*, *Aug. 29*, *2020*)

2) *12 missing*, *2 saved after boat sinks in Taiwan Straits*

(= *12 people missing*, *2 people saved after boat sinks in Taiwan Straits*)

船沉台湾海峡,12人失踪,2人被救

(*China Daily*, *Aug. 30*, *2020*)

3. Vividness

As an important part of a news report, news headlines are regarded as the advertisement of the news, which are used to indicate the theme of the news and attract readers. Most hurried readers always get the gist of the report by a glance at the headline and decide whether it is worth reading. If the headline is interesting, readers will be attracted to continue to read the news article. If the headline is dull, readers will probably give up the news story. As a result, in order to achieve vividness, journalists often make use of different techniques to add flavor to the language of the headline such as making some alterations in grammar and using rhetorical devices such as simile, metaphor, pun, hyperbole, parody, allusion, alliteration, antithesis, etc. For example:

1) Bush Builds <u>N</u>ew <u>B</u>ridges in Visit（metaphor）

2) Russian Reform：<u>Old Wine in New Bottle</u>（metaphor）

3) The Middle East，<u>the cradle of terrorism</u>（metaphor）

4) Records fell Like <u>Ripe Apples on a Windy Day</u>（simile）

5) Climbers Hold <u>Summit</u> Talks（pun）

6) <u>A Vow to Zip His Lips</u>（hyperbole）

7) <u>Queen Lear</u>（allusion）

8) <u>Measure for measure</u>（allusion）

9) <u>Britannia rues the waves</u>（parody）

10) <u>A Tale of Two Hearts</u>（parody）

11) <u>D</u>ecision and <u>d</u>ivision（alliteration）

12) <u>S</u>o Ordinary，<u>S</u>o Extraordinary（alliteration）

13) <u>S</u>oldiers，<u>S</u>alaries，<u>S</u>oar（alliteration）

14) <u>Tiny</u> Holes，<u>Big</u> Surgery（antithesis）

4.4.2 Translation of lexical items in English news headlines

1. Translation of acronym

(1) Transliteration

For example：

1) TOEFL，Chinese English language standards linked

（TOEFL：Test of English as a Foreign Language）

托福，中国英语能力等级标准对接

(China Daily，Dec. 12，2019)

2) OPEC 22nd Session Ends

（OPEC：Organization of Petroleum Exporting Countries Organization of Petroleum Exporting Countries，欧佩克：石油输出国组织）

欧佩克第 22 届分会落幕

(VOA，Apr. 10，2009)

(2) Translating out the full name

In view of the fact that not all acronyms can be translated according to the pronunciation, the translator had better translate the full name. For example：

1) Siemens ungags talking SMS

（SMS：Short Message Service，短信服务）

西门子发布手机语音短信服务

(The Register，Mar. 9，2005)

2) IMF urges US to postpone interest rate hike until 2016

（IMF：International Monetary Fund，国际货币基金组织）

国际货币基金组织希望美国将汇率上升推迟至 2016 年

(VOA，Jun. 6，2015)

3) *SpaceX craft safely brings NASA crew back home*
(NASA：*National Aeronautics and Space Administration* 美国国家航空航天局/美国宇航局；*SpaceX*：太空探索技术公司)
SpaceX 公司飞船将美国宇航局机组人员安全带回家

(*China Daily*，Aug. 4，2020)

4) *Ethical AI learns human rights framework*
(AI：*Artificial Intelligence*，人工智能)
人工智能学习人类道德框架

(*VOA*，Nov. 13，2019)

5) *START Announced to Begin in June on the 19th*
(START：*Strategic Arms Reduction Talks*，消减战略武器谈判)
消减战略武器谈判宣布 6 月 29 启动

(*VOA*，Jun. 20，2016)

(3) Shortening the full name in translation

Shortened forms, esp. those organizations or terms which are familiar to the public, are preferred in translation for the sake of saving space. For example：

1) *Captainless WTO sees no land in sight*
(WTO：*World Trade Organization*，世界贸易组织)
没有总干事的世贸组织看不到前景

(*China Daily*，Sept. 1，2020)

2) *EU recovery fund deal reached after marathon talks*
(EU：*European Union*，欧洲联盟)
经过马拉松式谈判，欧盟达成最大规模经济拯救计划

(*BBC*，Aug. 2，2020)

3) *Hollywood Helps CIA Come in From the Cold*
(CIA：*Central Intelligence Agency*，美国中央情报局)
好莱坞重塑中情局雄风

(*USA Today*，Feb. 20，2014)

2. Translation of new words in English news headlines

In order to draw close to the social life and grasp the times pulse, news report creates massive new words to reflect the new things, new thoughts, new phenomenon to attract readers' attention. Translators should try their best to find the nearest equivalent new expressions to bring freshness to the reader. For example：

1) *Martial arts fight cabin fever*
练武术对抗幽居病

(*China Daily*，Feb. 28，2020)

2) *2m UK jobs seen going after furlough scheme ends*
强制休假后，英国将失去 200 万个就业机会

(*China Daily*，Aug. 18，2020)

3) *Grain Sale Expected to Fall at Euromart*
(*Euromart*: *European Market*)
欧洲市场谷物价格有望下跌。

(*China Daily*, *Aug. 18*, *2016*)

4) *US Strives to Ease Stagflation*
(*Stagflation*: *Stagnation inflation*)
美国试图消除经济滞涨

(*Times*, *Aug. 18*, *2013*)

3. Translation of midget words

Midget words are verbs or nouns that are shorter with fewer syllables but more vivid used in news headlines to save space. For this phenomena, the translator should render it appropriately in Chinese. For example:

1) *Wearable tech aids stroke patients*
"可穿戴技术"助中风病人康复

(*BBC*, *Apr. 7*, *2018*)

2) *Ivorian Taekwondo Champions head to Rio Olympics*
科特迪瓦跆拳道冠军将进军里约奥运会

(*VOA*, *Jul. 9*, *2016*)

3) *With jobs cuts, New York is losing war of brooms*
纽约裁减清洁工,环境卫生恶化

(*The Wall Street Journal*, *Feb. 20*, *2004*)

4) *Quake death toll may top 2,000 (exceed)*
地震死亡人数超 2 000。

(*Daily Record*, *Mar. 2008*)

4. Omission of redundant words

First and foremost, the headline should be concise and brief to arouse readers' attention with terse and short words, so redundant words should be deleted in translation. For example:

Boris Johnson and Carrie Symonds announce birth of baby boy
Version A:鲍里斯·约翰逊和凯莉·西蒙兹宣布了一个男婴的诞生。
Version B:英国首相喜添贵子

(*BBC*, *May 3*, *2020*)

British Prime Minister Boris Johnson and his fiancée Carrie Symonds announced the birth of a healthy baby boy on May 3, 2020. This news headline listed both their names, which is clear but long. However, Chinese headline is preferred to be short and concise. The omission of the long names in Version B is obviously more idiomatic and eye-catching. In addition,"喜添贵子" is more in line with Chinese expressions in this case.

5. Using Short Form

1) *Frequency of China-US passenger flights will double*

Version A:中国美国客运航班班次将翻一番

Version B:<u>中美</u>客运航班班次将翻一番

(*China Daily*,Aug. 21,2020)

2) *Chinese Ship Hijacked in Indian Ocean*

Version A:中国船只在印度洋被劫持

Version B:<u>我船印度洋遭劫</u>

(*VOA*,Oct. 20,2009)

Both translations give the TT reader the information in the headline faithfully. The difference between the two is that Version B is much more polished than Version A. In translating the news headline, we choose the words with short form to save space, thus keeping conciseness in the headline.

4.4.3 Reproducing accuracy and clarity in news headlines

1. Addition

Chinese and English headlines are different. Firstly, Chinese news headlines are comparatively more specific than the English headlines by providing the subject or time or place, or other introductive and explanative information, though they are also required to be concise. Secondly, there is no formal change of tense in the Chinese language, so tense is usually not emphasized in the Chinese news headlines. Chinese uses auxiliaries (了、正在、将) to indicate that something happens in the past, the present or the future. Therefore, in E-C translation, the method of addition is often adopted to make the news more specific and clearer. For example:

1) *Stan Lee:Marvel Comics legend dies aged 95*

再见了,<u>漫威之父</u>！世间从此再无"彩蛋李"

(*BBC*,Nov. 13,2018)

Stan Lee is a comic master; however, many Chinese may not know him, so it is necessary to add "漫威之父" to explain whom Stan Lee is.

2) *Are cotton tote bags as good for the environment as we think?*

棉布手提袋真的那么环保吗？真相出乎意料

(*New York Times*,Jun. 12,2021)

In this version,"真相出乎意料" is added because the answer for the question is "no", which is out of people's expectation. The addition makes the news more attractive because readers may eager to know the fact and cannot help reading the news immediately.

3) *Trump Walks Out of Meeting After Democrats Refuse Border Wall Funding*

民主党拒绝拨款修墙,川普愤然离席

(*VOA*,Jan. 12,2019)

In this version,"愤然" is added based on the information in the body of the news, which vividly depicts the contradiction between Trump and the Democratic Party. Generally speaking, conflict can easily trigger readers' curiosity to read the news.

4) *Officials：Bin Laden Urged Followers to Attack US*
本·拉登在日志中敦促追随者攻击美国

(*VOA，May 13，2011*)

This news report was published after Osama Bin Laden's death. If the translator translates it word for word as "本·拉登敦促追随者攻击美国", it will confuse the readers because how can Osama Bin Laden urge his followers to attack the US since he is dead. Therefore, based on the content in the news body, "在日志中" is added to make it clear.

5) *Xi presides over meeting on Yellow River protection*
习近平主持召开黄河保护会议

(*China Daily，Aug. 31，2020*)

It is very common to use only the surname of a famous person in the English headlines. But when translating it into Chinese, the translator usually takes the target readers or China's actual conditions into account and provides the relevant information in the TL. Therefore, "Xi" is translated into "习近平".

6) *Tokyo organizers apologize for food waste, in latest Games headache.*
浪费！开幕式数千份食物无人吃被直接扔掉，东京奥组委发言人道歉

(*Reuters，Jul. 30，2021*)

In the translated version,"浪费" is added in the beginning of the sentence, because organizers of the Tokyo Olympics on Wednesday apologized for ordering too much food for their staff during the opening ceremony and letting it go to waste. The addition in the headline translation expresses the attitude of the public to the waste and make the news more sensational and attractive.

2. Adaptation

Since there are differences in the way of expressions between Chinese and English, it is impossible for translators to make a word for word translation. As a result, adaptation method is often employed to make the version conform to Chinese conventions. For example：

1) *And the Oscar Goes To …*
Version A：奥斯卡奖颁给……
Version B：奥斯卡奖花落谁家？

(*VOA，Feb. 21，2011*)

In the above example, both versions are accurate. However, Version B is in line with Chinese expression habit, thus more acceptable by Chinese readers.

2) *US "black lives matter" protests drive global online race debate*
Version A："黑人生命很重要"抗议推动全球网上种族辩论
Version B："黑人命也是命"激发全球网上种族辩论

(VOA, Aug. 10, 2020)

Both versions fully transmit the meaning of the original headline, while "黑人命也是命" in Version B is more idiomatic and it indicates black people's fight against race discrimination in the U.S.

3) The older, the wiser

Version A：越老，越明智，越冷静

Version B：人愈老，智愈高，心愈平

The news under such a headline focuses on the wisdom and calmness demonstrated in dealing with problems of all kinds by the senior citizens after their retirement. It is not wrong to translate the headline as what Version A does. However, Version B enhances the "sentiment" and "charm" of the TL more accurately, vividly and rhythmically.

(BBC, May 3, 2020)

Here list more examples：

- *Olympic Games Open with Rousing Romp Through British Life*
  "最炫英伦风"拉开伦敦奥运帷幕
- *Hangzhou is investing in becoming the esports capital of the world*
  杭州致力打造世界电竞之都
- *Job interview mistakes that you might not notice—but recruiters will*
  这些面试错误你可能意识不到，但是面试官很介意
- *A Mountain of Troubles*
  是非之地
- *Language Problems*
  都是语言惹的祸
- *Hard Times and a Bleak House*
  艰难时世和荒凉的议院
- *UK Writers Fly High On World Book Day*
  英国作家在"世界图书日"独领风骚
- *Climbers Hold Summit Talks*
  登山运动员会师峰顶
- *The Chinese market is a bottomless pit.*
  中国的市场无限广大。

3. Paraphrase

There are cases in which neither can we keep the meaning and the figure of speech at the same time, nor can we create a certain figure of speech in the TT to replace the one in the ST. What we have to do is to paraphrase the SL and transform the meaning intact into the TL. For example：

Japanese dash to US to say "I do"

The news under this headline is about some travel agents "new service of providing American wedding for Japanese". The phrase "I do" is a metaphor for western style wedding, in which both the bride and the groom will be asked to answer questions like "Do you take … to be your lawful wedded wife/husband to live together in the estate of matrimony?" with it. If we just literally translate it into "日本人涌往美国去说我愿意" to preserve the original figure of speech, the reader will be totally puzzled and misled. Considering the readability of the headline, we had better translate it into "日本情侣求浪漫喜事涌到美国办".

In another news report about American women bravely pursuing love but not wanting to get married, the headline is "Yes to Love, No to Marriage". With direct translation, the headline will be "对恋爱说是,对婚姻说不". This expression is understandable, but unable to stimulate the reader's interest in reading. Therefore, under the guidance of functional theory, it can be paraphrased and translated as "恋爱至上,拒绝围城", which is a good reflection of the news content, and it is more interesting.

4.4.4 Reproducing vividness

Good headlines add to stylistic elegance. In order to reproduce the vividness of the SL in the TL, the translator should refine and polish the language, i.e. "try every possible means to make use of the genius of the SL" (Liu,1998:19) and omit the redundant elements in the headline, produce an orderly layout and make use of the rhetorical device to reproduce the desired vividness.

In order to reproduce the informative and persuasive functions, the translator should translate the headlines in a creative way to reproduce its vividness in the TL.

1. Semantic translation

Semantic translation refers to a method to render of text from one language to another by following closely the form of the source language. It can provide fluent and accurate translation that is easily comprehended by the readers of the target language. As far as translation of rhetoric devices is concerned, semantic translation is the way to copy the figure of speech in the SL, because it could retain the "sentiment" and "charm" of the original. For example:

1) *Where there is smoke, there is cash*

The news report is about the status quo of production and sale of tobacco in America and exposes to the readers that it is the mutual interest between the tobacco companies and politicians that gives rise to rampant spread of cigarette-smoking. The headline is a parody of the proverb "Where there is smoke, there is fire", thus informing the reader of the infamous collusion between the two sides. As for this headline, we can simply imitate the original pattern and translate it into"哪里有烟,哪里就有钱". The following are more examples:

- *Russian Reform: Old Wine in New Bottle*
  俄罗斯改革:新瓶装旧酒
- *The Middle East, the cradle of terrorism*
  中东:恐怖主义的摇篮

Chapter Four Translation of News Report

- *Queen Lear*
  李尔"女王"
- *Measure for measure*
  以牙还牙
- *A Tale of Two Hearts*
  两颗心的故事
- *So Ordinary, So Extraordinary*
  既平凡,又脱俗
- *Tiny Holes, Big Surgery* (antithesis)
  小洞不补成大洞

In addition to rhetoric devices, many headlines can be translated semantically without changing the word order of the original sentences to keep the original style. For example:

- *Israel withdraws troops from Palestinian towns*
  以色列从巴勒斯坦撤军
- *Shanghai facing trade challenges from other areas*
  上海在贸易方面正面临其他地区的挑战
- *The Police Have Been Attacked in Clashes*
  警方在冲突中受到攻击
- *BBC Considering Starting Global Television Service*
  英国广播公司拟开通全球电视服务
- *Different Reward for Women's Labor*
  妇女同工不同酬
- *Deposits, Loans Rising in HK*
  存贷款额在港回升
- *US to Ease Technology Sale to China*
  美将简化对华科技销售

2. Communicative translation

More often than not, it is very difficult to keep both the meaning and the figure of speech in the TL. Under such circumstances, translators should take the method of communicative translation to create new headlines in Chinese to make the version idiomatic and vivid, because communicative method is suitable when the semantic translation is difficult to be understood or accepted by the readers or the translation seems not as attractive or powerful as the original text. For example:

1) *Red Envelopes Become Burden*
Version A:红包成为国庆负担
Version B:国庆节,婚礼红包劫

(*China Daily*, Sept. 26, 2019)

2) *Is "Globalization" helping or hurting?*
Version A:全球化是帮助还是伤害?

Version B：全球化:幸或者不幸?

(*Economics*, Feb. 12, 2020)

3) *5 Books About Love Everyone Should Read At Least Once*
Version A：五本关于爱情的书每个人至少应该读一次
Version B：五本关于爱情的图书:让我再浪漫一把!

(*Unipus*, Sept. 6, 2021)

4) *Van Goghes Recovered After the Theft*
Version A：梵高名画窃走后被找回
Version B：梵高名画 失而复得

(*highbeam.com*, 2012)

5) *culture and psychology：you are what you eat*
Version A：文化与心理:吃什么就长成什么样
Version B：文化与心理:一方水土养一方人

(*The Economist*, Feb. 21, 2015)

6) *Cheaper oil：winners and losers*
Version A：便宜石油:赢家和输家
Version B：油价暴跌:几家欢喜几家愁

(*Ecologist*, Oct. 31, 2014)

Compared the above Version A with Version B, though both translations convey the same meaning, Version Bs are much better. Version As seems to be dull and boring, while Version Bs not only embody the principle of clarity and infectivity in news headline translation, but also take full advantage of the charm of the TL, thus improving the novelty and readability of the headline.

In communicative translation, language forms often give way to function and purpose of the TL. Therefore, translators should liberate themselves from the rigid word for word translation and take appropriate methods such as division, restructuring and reversing to make the version smooth, understandable and attractive. The following are more examples.

- *Swimmer charged with assault kicked off Olympic team*
  泳将动粗 无缘北京
- *Lightning strikes twice*
  闪电再次划过,博尔特两项卫冕
- *Accuser accused*
  原告没告成,反而成被告
- *Corruption Reports Against Police Rise*
  警察腐败,怨声四起
- *Silent office workers demand to be heard*
  "不闻不问"的办公室员工 今后将不再不闻不问了
- *Chinese delegation first to win over 30 golds at Tokyo Olympics*
  中国军团领跑奥运会奖牌榜 田径项目创造历史

- *Trump offers mixed signals on possible closing of border with Mexico*
  是否要关美墨边界？特朗普发出含混信号
- *Scarlett Johansson sues Disney over "Black Widow" streaming release*
  寡姐起诉迪士尼：《黑寡妇》网播违反合约
- *Scientists based in Japan have successfully 3D printed a hunk of wagyu beef complete with marbling*
  日本研制出首款3D打印牛肉 "大理石花纹"以假乱真
- *Ask the Juggle: Job-hunting While Working Full-time*
  骑驴找马：如何在职找工作
- *No, honey is NOT as healthy as you thought*
  破除"蜂蜜迷信"：蜂蜜没有你想的那么健康

To sum up, headline translation is not an easy work, so translators should be flexible and creative by taking appropriate methods to deal with it.

4.5 Translation of News Lead

4.5.1 Comparison between Chinese and English news leads

News leads in both English and Chinese tend to give the gist, or the most important and essential information of the news report; that is, the five Ws and an H: *when, why, what, who, where* and *how*. In the English news lead, usually the news source "who said it" is put at the end while in the Chinese news lead, it is often put at the beginning. For example:

1) *Having proven to be a useful tool during the epidemic, online courses will continue to be provided to students alongside on-campus education, the Shanghai Municipal Education Commission announced on Aug. 31.*

8月31日，上海市教委宣布，疫情期间已得到肯定的在线课程将与线下教育结合，继续为学生提供教学服务。

(*China Daily, Sept. 2, 2020*)

2) *Beijing will gradually resume direct international flights starting Thursday, <u>China's top civil aviation watchdog said</u>.*

<u>中国民航总局表示</u>，北京将从周四开始逐步恢复国际直航。

(*China Daily, Sept. 2, 2020*)

3) *Despite bailouts for Greece, Ireland and Portugal, Europe's debt crisis may yet spread to core euro zone countries and emerging Eastern Europe, <u>the International Monetary Fund said on Thursday</u>.*

<u>国际货币基金组织周四称</u>：尽管援助了希腊、爱尔兰、葡萄牙，欧盟的债务危机依然可能会蔓延到欧元区核心的国家和新兴的东欧。

(*VOA, May 13, 2011*)

What's more, the ways to express the information differ much between English and

Chinese. English leads tend to squeeze all the information in a long and complicated sentence, but Chinese will express these factors in several short sentences. For example:

1) *The United States and China recently dispatched rovers to Mars, while the United Arab Emirates sent an orbiter to the red planet, where it is hoped humans one day will tread.*

中美最近都向火星发射了探测器,同时,阿联酋也向这颗红色星球发射了一颗人造卫星,希望有一天人类可以踏上这片土地。

(VOA, Aug. 3, 2020)

2) *Across the desert landscape of two grey hills New Mexico, a pickup truck brings food and firewood to a Navajo family of seven whose father died of the COVID-19 infection hours earlier.*

穿越新墨西哥州两座灰色山丘的沙漠景观,一辆小卡车把食物和柴火带给纳瓦霍人的一个七口之家。这家人的父亲几小时前死于新冠病毒。

(VOA, Jul. 24, 2020)

3) *WASHINGTON (Reuters) —President Barack Obama and congressional leaders reached a last-minute budget deal on Friday, averting a government shutdown that would have idled hundreds of thousands of federal workers.*

华盛顿(路透社)——本周五,总统奥巴马与国会领导人在最后一刻就预算方案达成了共识,从而避免了政府停工(危机),保障了成百上千联邦政府员工的生计。

(VOA, May 11, 2011)

4.5.2 Functionalist translation of news leads

Now that the lead is the core of a news story, it is important to translate it effectively and accurately. As we know, the summary lead is quite compact, which gives reader the main information of the news in just one sentence. We should render the information in the summary lead faithfully into the TT. In addition, the TT should conform to the habitual expressing way of the TT reader, i.e., the TT should make sense and be understandable. Because of the structural difference in English and Chinese leads, "communicative translation" that allows modification has greater practical significance than "semantic translation" to achieve the ideal "charm" of the original.

In order to translate the English sentence with hypotactic characteristics into the Chinese sentence with paratactic characteristics, we should first and foremost divide the English sentence into several sense groups, which could be a word, a phrase, a clause, or even a combination of any of them. After that, we can transform the sense groups into Chinese counterparts and at the same time reorder them according to Chinese norms of the sequence of time or the sequence of logic." (Jiang, 2002:14) In other words, in translating the summary lead, we should clarify the meaning groups contained in a sentence, find out the logical relationships among them, and reconstruct them in the paratactic form in Chinese.

Chapter Four Translation of News Report

It is well-known that each language has its own genius; that is, each language possesses its own distinctive characteristics in sentence building, word orders, techniques for linking clauses into sentences, etc. which should be recognized by the translator. Techniques applied in the translation of English news leads:

1. Analyzing the components of complicated English sentences

In order to convert English hypotactic structure into Chinese paratactic structure, we should first of all analyze the long sentences and then divide the sentences into several meaning groups for full understanding. For example:

Example 1

The Marvel star filed a lawsuit Thursday in Los Angeles Superior Court, alleging her contract was breached when the company released "Black Widow" on its streaming service Disney ＋ at the same time it debuted in theaters.

(*China Daily*, Jul. 30, 2021)

The news lead above contains the following information:

who: *The Marvel star*

what: *filed a lawsuit alleging her contract was breached* …

Where: *in Los Angeles Superior Court*

When: *Thursday*

Chinese version：7月29日,这位漫威明星向洛杉矶高等法院提起诉讼,指控该公司在《黑寡妇》在院线上映的同时,安排在其流媒体服务Disney＋上线,违反了合同。

Example 2

The Africa Centers for Disease Control and Prevention (Africa CDC) on Tuesday said that the death toll from the ongoing COVID -19 pandemic has climbed to 29,833 across the African continent as the number of positive cases rose to 1,252,552.

(*Xinhua*, Sept. 2, 2020)

The above lead contains the following information:

Who: *The Africa Centers for Disease Control and Prevention (Africa CDC)*

When: *on Tuesday*

What: *said that the death toll from the ongoing COVID -19 pandemic has climbed to 29,833 across the African continent*

Why: *as the number of positive cases rose to 1,252,552*

Chinese version：非洲疾控中心周二表示,随着阳性病例数上升至1 252 552例,目前非洲大陆流行的COVID-19造成的死亡人数已攀升至29 833人。

After analyzing the constituents of a long complicated sentence and dividing it into meaning groups to make the meaning clear, it is time to express it in idiomatic Chinese by taking different methods.

2. Translation techniques

(1) Keeping the original order

When the structure of the English sentence happens to be similar to the Chinese sentence, the original word order can be kept in translation.

Example 1

Global Times—Chinese State Councilor and Foreign Minister Wang Yi on Friday (French time) met with French President Emmanuel Macron during his ongoing European tour and the two discussed a wide range of topics including co-developing a COVID-19 vaccine and France's pledge not to ban Chinese tech company Huawei.

(*Jul. 1, 2020*)

《环球时报》——中国国务委员兼外交部长王毅本周五(法国时间)在欧洲访问期间会见了法国总统马克龙,双方讨论了广泛的话题,包括共同开发新冠肺炎疫苗,以及法国承诺不禁止中国科技公司华为。

Example 2

China Daily—Japan's Chief Cabinet Secretary Yoshihide Suga announced on Wednesday his bid to become the nation's next prime minister, saying he will continue "Abenomics" reforms.

(*Sept. 1, 2020*)

《中国日报》——日本内阁官房长官菅义伟周三宣布,他将竞选日本下一任首相,并称他会继续进行"安倍经济"改革。

(2) Rearranging the information sequence

As we have mentioned above, the leads of English news put the most valuable information at the very beginning, so the syntactic pattern is also determined by news value. "The lead sentence usually contains one idea and follows the subject-verb-object sentence structure for clarity." (Mencher, 2003: 111) In translating, we should spot the most important value and adjust the sequence of the information to make it conform to the features of Chinese news reporting.

Example 1

China Daily—Russia has expressed interest in cooperating with China and Huawei Technologies Co. on 5G technologies, Russian news agency TASS reported, amid intense US efforts to contain the Chinese telecom giant.

(*Aug. 28, 2020*)

俄罗斯已表示有兴趣与中国和华为技术有限公司开发5G技术,俄罗斯塔斯新闻社报道,同时,美国也在努力遏制中国电信巨头。

Obviously, this translation does not conform to the habitual Chinese expression. Thus we can rearrange the sequence of information at the expense of the original syntactic pattern as follows:

据俄罗斯塔斯社报道,俄方已表示有兴趣在5G技术开发方面与中国和华为技术公司合作。与此同时,美国正在加紧努力遏制中国电信巨头。

Chapter Four Translation of News Report

Example 2

China Daily—The Intermediate People's Court in Hulunbuir, North China's Inner Mongolia autonomous region, is investigating a case in which an inmate was allegedly released on parole for medical services and didn't serve his prison term, Beijing News reported on Friday.

(Sept. 4, 2020)

The original word order:

①*The Intermediate People's Court in Hulunbuir,*

②*North China's Inner Mongolia autonomous region,*

③*is investigating a case*

④*in which an inmate was allegedly released on parole for medical services and didn't serve his prison term,*

⑤*Beijing News reported on Friday.*

If translated literally, the word order would be:

①内蒙古呼伦贝尔市中级人民法院，

②中国内蒙古自治区，

③正在调查一起案件，

④一个囚犯保外就医而未服刑，

⑤周五北京新闻报道。

If this news lead is translated according to the original word order, it would sound awkward, so the sentence structure should be adjusted as follows.

据《新京报》周五报道，中国北方内蒙古自治区呼伦贝尔市中级人民法院正在调查一起囚犯保外就医而获得假释未服刑的案件。

Example 3

CNN – In an incident that is another major embarrassment to Israel's once-feared Mossad Intelligence agency, Swiss authorities on Thursday that a suspected Israeli secret agent had been placed under arrest and four others were being sought, after an illegal bugging operation was uncovered by police.

(Nov. 13, 2018)

The original word order:

① *In an incident that is another major embarrassment to Israel's once-feared Mossad Intelligence agency,*

② *Swiss authorities on Thursday that a suspected Israeli secret agent had been placed under arrest*

③ *and four others were being sought,*

④ *after an illegal bugging operation was uncovered by police.*

If translated literally, the word order would be:

①这是对令人一度恐惧的以色列摩萨德情报机构的又一重大尴尬事件,

②瑞士当局星期四宣布,逮捕了一名被疑为以色列特工的人,

③另有四人目前正被追捕,

④警方在破获一起非法窃听案件后。

The rearranged sentence which is readable to the Chinese is as follows:

瑞士当局星期四宣布,警方在破获一起非法窃听案件后,逮捕了一名以色列特工嫌疑人,另有四人目前正在追捕中。这一事件使得曾不可一世的以色列摩萨德情报局再次大为尴尬。

Example 4

Lead:HONG KONG,April 28(Reuters)— Hong Kong shares are seen recovering and edging higher on Thursday morning following strong quarterly results from two Chinese banks and after the U.S. Federal Reserve signaled it would retain its ultra-loose monetary policy.

(Apr. 28,2016)

The original word order:

① *Hong Kong shares are seen recovering and edging higher on Thursday morning*

② *following strong quarterly results from two Chinese banks*

③ *and after the U.S. Federal Reserve signaled*

④ *it would retain its ultra-loose monetary policy.*

If translated literally, the word order would be:

① 香港股票似乎有被恢复和缓慢上涨的势头在周四早上

② 随着中国两家银行的强大的季度业绩

③ 在美国联邦储备委员会示意

④ 要保持松散货币政策后。

Obviously, the word order is not accordant with the semantic logic of Chinese expression, so it should be rearranged like this:

香港,4月28日(路透社)——随着中国两家银行的强大季度业绩和在美国联邦储备委员会示意会保持松散货币政策后,周四早上香港股票似乎有恢复和缓慢上涨的势头。

Example 5

ISLAMABAD,May 13(Reuters)—The death toll from a suicide bombing at a northwest Pakistan paramilitary force academy on Friday, the first major attack by suspected militants since Osama Bin Laden was killed in the country on May 2, has climbed to at least 69, a police official said.

(May 13,2019)

The original word order:

① *The death toll from a suicide bombing at a northwest Pakistan paramilitary force academy on Friday,*

② *the first major attack by suspected militants*

③ since Osama Bin Laden was killed in the country on May 2,
④ has climbed to at least 69, a police official said.
If translated literally, the word order would be:
① 发生在本周五巴基斯坦西北部准军事部队学院一宗自杀式爆炸袭击的人数,
② 第一次大规模的一次袭击案
③ 自拉登 3 月 2 日在巴基斯坦遇袭之后,
④ 据一名官员透露,死亡人数至少达到了 69 人

The rearranged translation which is readable to the Chinese is as follows:

伊斯兰堡(路透社)——本周巴基斯坦西北部准军事部队学院发生了一宗自杀式爆炸事件。这是自拉登 3 月 2 日在巴基斯坦遇袭之后恐怖组织实施的规模最大的一次袭击案。据一名官员透露,死亡人数至少达到了 69 人。

(3) Adjusting the voice

As for the voice of the sentences in the news leads, it can be either active or passive, and sometimes mixed together. Generally speaking, the active voice appears more often than passive voice, but it is also true that passive voice appears more often in English leads than in Chinese leads. In translating, we should adjust the passive voice if necessary to make the translation more readable and acceptable to the Chinese readers.

Example 1

A blue whale has been spotted off the coast of Sydney in Australia for possibly only the third time in almost 100 years, wildlife authorities say.

野生动物当局称,在澳大利亚悉尼海岸附近发现一头蓝鲸。这可能是近百年来的第三次。

(BBC, Sept. 4, 2020)

Example 2

The city's subways and buses have been disinfected daily for months, but ridership on subways is down by 75 percent.

几个月来,纽约市的地铁和公交车每天都要消毒,但地铁的乘客人数下降了 75%。

(China Daily, Sept. 4, 2020)

Example 3

A water-proof drone is being used by Australian scientists to collect the highly-treasured nasal mucus of migrating whales. The snot is rich with fresh DNA, viruses and bacteria, and *is collected* by a drone that hovers over the blowholes of humpback whales as they embark on their epic annual journey along Australia's east coast. From Sydney, Phil Mercer reports.

(VOA, May 5, 2019)

菲尔·默瑟从悉尼报道,澳大利亚科学家正在使用一种防水无人机收集迁徙鲸鱼的珍贵鼻黏液。这种鼻涕富含新鲜的 DNA、病毒和细菌,当座头鲸沿着澳大利亚东海岸展开史诗般的年度旅行时,悬停在其气孔上方的无人机就能收集这种鼻涕。

Example 4

15-year-old student opened fire at his high school in the American state of Michigan, killing four students and injuring seven on Tuesday. Local government lawyers announced Wednesday that the student, Ethan Crumbley, <u>will be charged</u> with murder and terrorism.

周二,一名 15 岁的学生在其就读的美国密歇根州的一所高中开枪,造成 4 名学生死亡、7 人受伤。当地政府律师周三宣布,这名名叫伊桑·克伦布利的学生将以谋杀和恐怖主义罪名<u>受到起诉</u>。

(VOA, Dec. 4, 2021)

To some extent, "To translate is to communicate." (Pattanaik, 1994:142) To achieve this aim satisfactorily, translators must respect the genius of the two languages in translation. "Rather than force the formal structure of one language upon another, the effective translator must be quite prepared to make any and all formal changes necessary to reproduce the message in the distinctive structural forms of the receptor language." (Nida, 1969:4)

Chapter Five Business English Translation

With the rapid development of economic globalization, the trade between China and the world is becoming very frequent. Many multinational companies come to China to build factories, and many local enterprises expand their businesses to overseas markets. As an international language, English has become a bridge of international business and trade. Therefore, the demand for business English translation in China has greatly increased.

5.1 Definition of Business English

International business consists of a wide range of activities from marketing, import and export, international finance, business management to company operation and logistics management. It covers all business activities relating to the transfer of products, labor, and capital as well as other economic resources.

Business English is the product of the worldwide business and trade. It is a dynamic notion with an increasingly large, expanding and innovative connotation. As for non-English speaking countries, business English is a cross-subject, namely, a combination of language media and a specialized subject.

International business English focuses on specific communication requirements for business affairs which are dealt with in companies, factories and related industries such as banking, insurance, finance, logistics, and transportation which involves import and export trade, international technology transfer, international labor cooperation, etc. Since business English includes a variety of texts which form a big spectrum, it is not easy to elaborate on the translation of every types. For this reason, this chapter will focus on the translation of business English in its written form confined to business contracts and business letters.

5.2 Linguistic and Stylistic Features of Business English

As an English for special purpose, business English has its distinctive characteristics which differentiate it from general English. Business language is legal, professional, formal, unadorned and frozen, which is demonstrated in its choice of words and sentence patterns.

5.2.1 Lexical features

1. Terminology

Compared with general English, business English has more professional orientation and covers a wide range of business activities including accounting, law, advertising, insurance, finance, engineering, management, trade, etc. which have their own special expressions. Meanwhile, there are many semi-professional vocabulary which are transformed from ordinary vocabulary and have special meanings in business English. This type of vocabulary accounts for a large part in business English, and most of them are polysemy. The large number of terminology and semi-professional words may present obstacles for translators, so it is crucial to master such technical terms in translation.

The following are some highly directional normative words that often appear in business English.

(1) Terminology on import and export

export credit 出口信贷
export subsidy 出口津贴
dumping 商品倾销
exchange dumping 外汇倾销
special preferences 优惠关税
bonded warehouse 保税仓库
trade surplus 贸易顺差
import licence 进口许口证
export licence 出口许口证
trade deficit 贸易逆差
import quotas 进口配额制
free trade zone 自由贸易区
value of foreign trade 对外贸易值
value of international trade 国际贸易值
generalized system of preferences 普遍优惠制
most favored nation treatment 最惠国待遇

(2) Terminology on price

freight 运费
wharfage 码头费
total value 总值
landing charges 卸货费
customs duty 关税
stamp duty 印花税
net price 净价
price including commission 含佣价
port dues 港口税
return commission 回佣
discount, allowance 折扣
retail price 零售价
inquiry 询盘
quotation 报价
counter offer 还盘
reference price 参考价
current price 现行价格(时价)
spot price 现货价格
forward price 期货价格
International Market price 国际市场价格
FOB—free on board 离岸价(船上交货价)
irrevocable documentary L/C 不可撤销跟单信用证
confirmed L/C 保兑信用证
bank draft 银行汇票
commercial draft 商业汇票
date draft/time draft 远期汇票
acceptance draft 承兑汇票

arrival draft 到货汇票
clean draft 光票；普通汇票
exercise price 敲定价格
forward exchange 远期外汇交易
transaction 交易
direct draft 直接汇票
documentary draft 押汇汇票（交换提单的汇票）
telegraphic draft 电汇票
tenor draft 限期汇票
three party draft 三方汇票
two party draft 双方汇票
draft for collection 托收汇票
letter of credit (L/C) 信用证
documentary credit 跟单信用证
clean credit 光票信用证
revocable credit 可撤销信用证
unconfirmed L/C 不保兑信用证
sight letter of credit 即期信用证
usance letter of credit 远期信用证

transferable L/C 可转让信用证
non-transferable L/C 不可转让信用证
revolving credit 循环信用证
standby letter of credit 备用信用证
applicant for the credit 开证申请人
the issuing bank 开证行
advising bank 通知行
transmitting bank 转证行
confirming bank 保兑行
beneficiary 受益人
bill of exchange 汇票
commercial invoice 商业发票
insurance policy 保单
beneficiary's certificate 受益人证明书
inspection certificate 检验证书
remittance 汇付
spot exchange transaction 即期外汇交易
strike price 协议价格
dishonored 退票，拒付
accept 兑现，承付

(3) Terminology on delivery

delivery 交货
shipment 装运，装船
charter (the chartered ship) 租船
time of delivery 交货时间
voyage charter 定程租船
time of shipment 装运期限
time charter 定期租船
shipper, consignor 托运人（一般指出口商）
consignee 收货人
regular shipping liner 班轮
lighter 驳船
tanker 油轮
shipping space 舱位
clearance of goods 报关
cargo receipt 陆运收据
to take delivery of goods 提货
airway bill 空运提单

certificate of origin 产地证明书
P/L 装箱
packing list 装箱单
bill of lading 提单
optional port 选择港（任意港）
optional charges 选港费
immediate shipments 立即装运
prompt shipments 即期装运
shipments within 30 days after receipt of L/C 收到信用证后30天内装运
partial shipment not allowed or permitted partial 不允许分批装船
shipment during January or January shipment 一月份装船
shipment during… in two lots 在……（时间）分两批装船

shipment during… in two equal lots 在……(时间)平均分两批装船
in three monthly shipments 分三个月装运
in three equal monthly shipments 分三个月，每月平均装运

port of destination 目的港
port of shipment 装运港
port of discharge 卸货港
inspection certification 检验检疫证书

(4) Terminology on negotiation and contract signing

party 当事人/签订合同的一方
approve 允许，批准
as from 自……日起
as per/in accordance with/subject to 按照，根据
assign/transfer 转让
authority 权力
commence 开始
construe 解释
in lieu of 代替
interim/temporary 临时
obligation/liability 责任，义务
pertaining to/in respect to 关于……
purchase/procure 购买
require/request 请求，申请
revise/rectify 纠正，改正
said above 上述
supplement/add 增加，添加
terminate/conclude/expire 结束，终止
variation/alteration/modification 改变
arbitration 仲裁
termination 终止

force majeure 不可抗力
jurisdiction 管辖
futures 期货
firm (definite) offer 实盘
non-firm (indefinite) offer 虚盘
offeror 发盘人
offeree 收盘人
bid/bidding 递盘
bid firm 递实盘
usual practice 习惯做法
policy 保险单
documentary 跟单
liability/obligation 责任，义务
business negotiation 交易磋商
subject to our final confirmation 需经我方最后确认
time of validity 有效期限
general terms and conditions 一般交易条款和条件
purchase contract 购买合同
sales contract 销售合同
purchase confirmation 购货确认书
sales confirmation 销售确认书
subject to seller's confirmation 需经卖方确认

(5) Terminology on trade mode

consignment 寄售
auction 拍卖
invitation of tender 招标
submission of tender 投标
agent 一般代理人

general agent 总代理人
agency agreement 代理协议
distribution 分销，销售
accumulative commission 累计佣金
processing on giving materials 来料加工

assembling on provided parts 来料装配
exclusive right 独家经营/专营权
exclusivity agreement 独家经营/包销/代理协议
sole agency/exclusive agency 独家代理
acquire 收购

(6) Terminology on quality

quality 品质
original sample 原样
duplicate sample 复样
counter sample 对等样品
reference sample 参考样品
sealed sample 封样
representative sample 代表性样品
specifications 规格
standard type 标准
article No. 货号
catalogue 商品目录
pamphlet 宣传小册

(7) Terminology on inspection and arbitration

claim 索赔
disputes 争议
penalty 罚金条款
arbitration 仲裁
Force Majeure 不可抗力
arbitral tribunal 仲裁庭
inspection certificate of quality 品质检验证书
right of recourse 追索权
reimbursement draft 索偿汇票
factoring 保理
inspection certificate of weight (quantity) 重量检验证书
commodity inspection bureau 商品检验局
net weight 净重
capacity 容积
gross for net 以毛作净
volume 体积
gross weight 毛重

(8) Terminology on foreign exchange

foreign exchange 外汇
devaluation 法定贬值
foreign currency 外币
revaluation 法定升值
rate of exchange 汇率
floating rate 浮动汇率
hard currency 硬通货
soft currency 软通货
direct quotation 直接标价
indirect quotation 间接标价
gold parity 金平价
gold standard 金本位制度
buying rate 买入汇率
selling rate 卖出汇率
fixed rate 固定汇率
paper money system 纸币制度
international monetary fund 国际货币基金
gold and foreign exchange reserve 黄金外汇储备
official upper and lower limits of fluctuation 汇率波动的官定上下限

2. Archaisms

Many terms used in business contract English are derived from Latin or French with the same prefix or suffix. The meanings are relatively stable and conducive to the accurate expression of concepts. For example, "ad valorem duty" [Latin, 从价（关）税], "bona fide holder" Latin, 汇票的善意持有人, "pro rata tax rate" Latin, 即 proportional tax rate, 比例税率, "insurance premium per capita" (Latin, 人均保险费), force majeure (French, 不可抗

力），Pro forma（Latin，估算表）.

Business Contract English has the characteristics of classical style. One of the main signs of this style is the use of archaism which has distinctive stylistic color. Although archaic words are rarely used in modern spoken English and general written language, they appear in a large number in legal texts such as business contracts, which fully reflects its solemn and serious style. Contract English has many distinctive compound adverbs composed of free morphemes "where", "here" and "there" combined with prepositions "in", "by", "with" and "after".

(1) here + prepositions: such as "hereto", "hereof", "herein", "hereafter", etc., of which "here" is equivalent to "this", referring to this document, contract or relevant documents.

(2) There + prepositions: such as "thereto", "thereon", "therein", "thereof", etc. of which "there" is equivalent to "that", which refers to a noun or noun phrase that has appeared in front of the sentence. Therefore, "thereto" means "to that".

(3) Where + preposition: such as "whereby", "wherein", "whereof", "whereupon" of which "Where" is equivalent to "which" or "what". Therefore, "where of" means "of which". For example, "payment in respect thereof" means "关于此项的付款".

The use of archaic words not only reflects its seriousness, but also avoids unnecessary repetition and makes the meaning clearer and concise. For example, "依照本合同相关规定" is hardly translated as "according to relevant terms and conditions in the contract" in English. Instead, it is often translated as "pursuant to provisions contained herein" or "as provided herein". As for "合同任何一方当事人不得转让本合同", "Neither party hereto may assign this contract" is used instead of "Neither party to the contract may assign this contract".

3. Auxiliary verbs

The meaning boundary of modal verbs in contract English is very clear, which reflects the preciseness of contract language. "Shall" is widely used in business contract English, which means "this clause is mandatory as stipulated by law". Its meaning is equivalent to "must", but "must" cannot be used in the contract. For example, "The seller shall present the following shipping documents to the bank for negotiation of L/C" indicates that "when negotiating the letter of credit with the bank, the seller must fulfill the legal obligation of submitting the required shipping documents, and shall ensure that the documents are consistent, otherwise the bank can refuse payment." "Will" only refers to the description of a certain proposal of one party to the contract or the behavior of a third party to the contract which does not constitute a legal constraint. "Should" has a subjective meaning, indicating "it's better to do so". "May" means "can", but in the contract, it is used instead of "can", because the former is more formal than the latter.

4. Juxtaposition of synonyms or related words

There is juxtaposition of words in business contract English, that is, synonyms or related words are often used in conjunction with "and" or "or". For example:

any and all 全部
any duties, obligations or liabilities 所有责任
laws, regulations and rules 法律法规
charges, fees, costs and expenses 各种费用
covenants and agreements 合同,协议
customs and usages 惯例
free and clear of 无
import duty and tax 进口税捐
secret and confidential 保密
packing and wrapping expenses 包装费
by and between 由双方……

rights and interests 权益
claims and debts 债权债务
ships and vessels 船只
sign and issue 签发
support and maintenance 维护
use and wont 习惯,惯例
injury or damage 损害
neglect or omit 忽略
terms and conditions 条款
fulfill or perform 履行
transferable or assignable 可转让的
null and void 无法律效力的
in full force and effect 完全有效

This parallel use of words makes the meaning of two or more words jointly define their meaning so as to eliminate the possible ambiguity caused by the polysemy of a word in a contract because the accuracy and preciseness of the contract determine that even small mistakes or omissions are not allowed.

In summary, the knowledge of lexical features of business English can help the translators read, understand and translate contracts accurately and effectively to avoid unnecessary disputes and finally promote the exchange and cooperation in international trade.

5.2.2 Syntactic features of business English

1. Long complex sentences

The syntax of business English is characterized by rigorous structure and long complex sentences with many additional elements such as adverbial clauses and attributive clauses to explain, limit or supplement the meaning of the main sentence. This not only reflects the solemn style and clear logic of a sentence, but also can eliminate the possibility of disputes caused by misinterpretation and misunderstanding, and safeguard the legitimate rights and interests of both parties.

Example 1

CTOR selects the compensation method described in Paragraph 2.2.1 of the "Attachment V: Subcontract Price and Payment Provisions" as a basis of compensation, subcontractor shall provide contractor, along with the Change Order Price Proposal, a sufficiently detailed breakdown of the proposed Change Order Price along with copies of all related Vendor/Subcontractor quotations for the materials/equipment added or any amount of discount or rebate subcontractor would receive from Vendor(s)/Subcontractor (s), directly or indirectly, for the said materials/equipment and the cost to be ultimately incurred by subcontractor, directly or indirectly, after all direct and indirect discounts and/or rebates to subcontractor.

This contract clause, 10 lines long, is characterized by complexity, which stipulates that the subcontractor has to provide all relevant papers and evidences in order to claim for compensation on account of Change Orders. The complex sentence is composed of a main clause with five paralleled objects combined by such connecters as "along with", "and", "or". The modifier "directly or indirectly" is used as many as three times to make the idea clearly expressed.

Example 2

If a Party breaches any of the representations or warranties given by it in Articles 18.1 or repeated in 18.2, then in addition to any other remedies available to the other Party under this contract or under Applicable Laws, it shall indemnify and keep indemnified the other Party and the company against any losses, damages, costs, expenses, liabilities and claims that such Party or the Company may suffer as a result of such breach.

This is also a long complex sentence with a conditional adverbial clause at the beginning of the sentence and a main clause "it shall indemnify and keep indemnified the other Party and the company against any losses, damages, costs, expenses, liabilities and claims" followed by an attributive clause "that such Party or the Company may suffer as a result of such breach".

2. Passive voice

R. Quirk (1985:105) points out, generally speaking, active voice is more common in English than passive voice, but there is considerable variation as to individual texts. Passive has been found to be ten times more frequent in informative texts such as scientific articles and business English because it has the function of objectivity and formality. For example,

1) A lease contract <u>shall be signed</u> for leasing the right to the use of the land by and between the lessor and the lessee.

2) In this author's opinion, safeguard rules <u>can be made and applied</u> by and between the members of the RTA, but the application requirements should be stricter than those in the safeguards of WTO.

3) The business of the Joint Venture Company shall not <u>be interrupted</u> or the organizational structure <u>be affected</u> during the assignment. After assignment has taken place, registration procedures for changes shall <u>be conducted</u> with the Administrative Bureau for Industry and Commerce within thirty (30) days.

To summarize, complex sentences take up a big proportion in business English for the purpose of precise and exact expression and passive expressions appear frequently for formality and objectivity.

5.3 Contract Translation

5.3.1 Definition of a contract

A contract is an overwhelmingly important part of international trade as contracts stipulate the work scope, rights and obligations of different parties. A contract is a formal written agreement, having the force of law, between two or more people or groups (by *Longman Dictionary of Contemporary English*). Contracts refer to agreements establishing, modifying and terminating the civil rights and obligations between subjects of equal footing, that is, between natural persons, legal persons or other organizations. In some sense, the signing of a contract is the first and foremost step in a trade.

5.3.2 Function of a contract and translation principle

According to Skopo stheorie, the strategies taken in any translation must be consciously and persistently in conformance with the function of the target text. As is mentioned above, the function of a contract is to regulate the rights, obligations and responsibilities of the parties accurately and strictly because it is a legal document that the parties involved shall comply with and it is the basic reference of solution to any dispute that may arise. Therefore, the first principle to be observed in contract translation is loyalty and accuracy, expressiveness and smoothness. In other words, the translator should consider the expectations and reading habit of the readers, use concise and professional language to transmit the information precisely and correctly. Otherwise, it may lead to difficulties in performing the contract and even dispute may arise.

5.3.3 Translation of terminology

In business texts, a large number of ordinary English words are given "business meaning", forming professional or semi-professional words. Such words are difficult to identify and easy to confuse, which brings great difficulties to translation. Therefore, translators should identify the meaning of the words according to the context and render them accurately and professionally. The following are some examples.

Example 1

balance 平衡,余额,结欠

The ordinary meaning for "balance" is "平衡", while in Business English, it may mean "余额","结余" or "结欠","差额".

 e.g. 1. ST: He accumulated a healthy <u>balance</u> with the saving bank.
    TT: 他在银行积累了不少的<u>结余</u>。
 e.g. 2. ST: The holiday <u>balance</u> must be paid by 8 weeks before departure.

TT：度假应付费用的差额必须在离开前8周付清。

Example 2

security 安全；担保，抵押品；证券

e.g.1. ST：He gave his house as a security.

TT：他以房子做抵押。

e.g.2. ST：Treasury securities are revalued daily.

TT：国债每天都在重新估价。

Example 3

floating 不固定的，浮动的

e.g.1. ST：It is not surprising that the world saw a return to a floating exchange rate system.

TT：在这种情况下，世界各国又恢复浮动汇率就不足为奇了。

e.g.2. ST：Floating policy is of great importance for export trade.

TT：统保单对出口贸易极为重要。

Example 4

confirm 证实，确认；批准（职位、协议等），认可

e.g.1. ST：We'd like to inform you that our counter sample will be sent to you by DHL by the end of this week and please confirm it ASAP so that we can start our mass production.

TT：很高兴通知您，我们的回样将于本周末用特快专递给您，请尽快确认，以便我们开始大批生产。

e.g.2. ST：Payment will be made by 100% confirmed, irrevocable Letter of Credit available by sight draft.

TT：付款方式为100%保兑、不可撤销信用凭证。

Example 5

negotiable 可商议的；流通的；可转让的；可兑现的

e.g.1. ST：Part-time barman required. Hours and salary negotiable.

TT：需要兼职酒吧招待。工作时间和薪水可以协商。

e.g.2. ST：This Bill of Lading is issued in a negotiable form, so it shall constitute title to the goods and holder by endorsement of this B/L.

TT：本提单以可转让的形式签发，因此经过背书后即可将所有权转让给他人。

Example 6

discount 打折扣；认为……不重要；对……不全信；低估；贴现

e.g.1. ST：You may get a 5% discount if your group is on a regular basis.

TT：如果你方定期给我方下订单，你方便可得到5%的折扣。

e.g.2. ST：If a seller extends credit to a time draft, they have made a trade acceptance. The seller can request that the bank finance the transaction by buying the draft. The bank is said to discount the draft.

TT：如卖方开出的是远期汇票，以此向买方提供信用，他们就已经开出商业承兑

汇票。卖方可以请银行买下商业承兑汇票。这就意味着银行对该汇票贴现了。

Example 7

endorse 背书；(公开)赞同,支持；认可；(在广告中)宣传,代言(某一产品)；(在支票背面)签名；(在驾驶执照上)记录违章事项

 e. g. 1. ST：Our products have been endorsed by the National Quality Inspection Association.

  TT：我们的产品为全国质量检查协会的推荐产品。

 e. g. 2. ST：Draft must be accompanied by full set original on board marine Bill off Lading made out to order, endorsed in blank, marked freight prepaid.

  TT：汇票必须附有全套正本已装船海运提单、凭指示、空白背书,注明运费预付。

Example 8

tender 提议；提供；提出；投标

 e. g. 1. ST：Under CIF, it is the seller's obligation to tender the relative documents to the buyer to enable him/her to obtain delivery of the goods or to recover for the loss, if they are lost on the voyage.

  TT：在 CIF 价格术语项下,卖方的责任是向买方递交有关单证,使其能在货物到达后提取货物；如果货物在运输途中丢失了,买方也可凭单证获取补偿。

 e. g. 2. ST：He became as exhilarated as if his tender for building a mansion had been accepted.

  TT：他兴高采烈,好像他承办大厦建筑的投标被接受了。

Example 9

entertain 招待,款待；使快乐；考虑

 e. g. ST：At present, we cannot entertain your counter offer, as our price quite reasonable.

  TT：我们的价格目前定得相当合理,故目前不考虑贵方的还盘。

Example 9

establish 建立,创立；查实；开出

 e. g. ST：We insist that you should keep your word by establishing the relevant L/C on time.

  TT：我们坚持你方应该信守承诺,按时开出信用证。

Example 10

enquiry 询问；查询；调查,探究；询盘

 e. g. ST：Should you find interest in any of the terms in our catalogue please do not hesitate to send your enquiries.

  TT：如对目录中的任何项目感兴趣,请直接寄来询盘。

5.3.4 Translation of archaisms

Archaisms such as *hereafter*, *hereby*, *herein*, *hereinafter*, *hereinbefore*, *hereof*, *hereto*, *hereunder*, *hereupon*, *herewith*, *thereafter*, *thereby*, *therefrom*, *therein*, *thereinafter*,*thereinbefore*,*thereon*,*thereof*,*thereunder*,*thereupon*,*therewith*,*whereby*,*whereof*,*whereto* are frequently used in English contract to avoid repetition and make the expression concise. Correct translation of such classical words can guarantee accurate information transmission. For example:

(1) ST: This Contract is made and signed in Shanghai on November 12, 2019, by and between AA Corporation (hereinafter referred to as the Seller) and BB Corporation (hereinafter referred to as the Buyer). The Buyer hereby orders from the Seller the following goods subject to the following conditions.

TT: 本合同由 AA 公司(以下称卖方)和 BB 公司(以下称买方)于 2019 年 11 月 12 日在上海签订。买方向卖方订购下列商品,条件如下。

Analysis: The adverb "here" is used as a prefix, and "hereinafter" means "later in this Contract"(在下文,以下), and "hereby" means "by this"(因此). It can be omitted in translation in this case.

(2) ST: The undersigned hereby certify that the goods to be supplied are made in USA.

TT: 下列签署人兹保证所供应之货物系在美国国内制造。

Analysis: "hereby" is translated as "兹". This word is often used in Chinese business contracts, which is in line with the stylistic characteristics of legal documents. The other two old style words "之" and "系" show the typical characteristics of formal and compact features of contract language style.

(3) ST: In case Party A shall decide not to continue the progress of Works, this Contract shall be terminated under Article 10 hereof.

TT: 如果甲方决定不再继续施工,本合同应按合同第 10 条的规定立即终止。

Analysis: "hereof" means "of this Contract"(关于此点,在本文中). It is omitted in the translation.

(4) ST: This contract shall be in duplicate to be held each by the Partie hereto and shall have two copies each kept by the Parties hereto for record.

TT: 本合同一式两份,合同双方各执一份,并各保留两份复印件,供双方存档。

Analysis: "hereto" means "to this"; "the Parties hereto" means "the Parties to this Contract". It is omitted in the translation.

(5) ST: The titles to the articles are for convenience of reference only, not part of this contract and shall not in any way effect the interpretation thereof.

TT: 本章程的标题仅供参考,不属于本合同的一部分,且不得以任何方式影响对本合同的解释。

Analysis: "thereof" means "of that", "of the said contract", translated as "本合同的".

(6) ST: The headings and marginal notes in these conditions shall not be deemed part thereof or be taken into consideration in the interpretation or construction thereof or of the Contract.

TT: 合同条件(条款)中的标题及旁注不应视为条款的一部分,在合同条条款或合同本身的解释中也不应加以考虑。

Analysis: "thereof" means "of these conditions"; "construction thereof" means "interpretation of these conditions", translated as "条款的".

(7) ST: "Temporary Works" means all temporary works of every kind (other than Contractor's Equipment) required in or about the execution and completion of the Works and the remedying of any defects therein.

TT: "临时工程"指在工程施工、竣工及修补工程中有任何缺陷时需要或有关的所有各种临时工程(承包人设备除外)。

Analysis: "therein" means "in that; in that particular context; in that respect". "any defects therein" means "any defects in the Works". It is omitted in the translation.

(8) ST: Instructions for the issuance of credits, the credits themselves, instructions for any amendment thereto and the amendments themselves shall be complete and precise.

TT: 开立信用证的指示、信用证本身、有关对信用证修改的指示以及其修改书本身,必须完整、明确。

Analysis: "any amendment thereto" means "any amendment to the credit", translated as "对信用证修改的".

(9) ST: Whereby the Buyers agree to buy and the Sellers agree to sell the undermentioned goods subject to the terms and conditions as stipulated hereinafter.

TT: 兹经买卖双方同意按照以下条款由买方购进,卖方售出以下商品。

Analysis: "whereby" means "by this contract", translated as "兹"; "hereinafter" means "in the following part", translated as "以下".

5.3.5 Translation of Auxiliary verbs

As is mentioned above, auxiliary verbs are widely used in business contract English. *May*, *shall*, *should*, *will* are very common, but these words have special meanings in the contract, so they should be translated with great caution to avoid disputes. "shall" means "must", and "will" refers to the description of a certain proposal of one party to the contract or the behavior of a third party to the contract which does not constitute a legal constraint. "Should" indicates a suggestion or instructional requirements "you'd better do sth.", and "may" means "can", but in the contract, it is used instead of "can", because the former is more formal than the latter. For example:

(1) ST: The parties hereto shall, first of all, settle any dispute arising from or in connection with the contract by friendly negotiations. Should such negotiations fail, such dispute may be referred to the People's Court having jurisdiction on such dispute for settlement in the absence of any arbitration clause in the disputed contract or in default of agreement reached after such dispute occurs.

TT: 双方首先应通过友好协商,解决因合同而发生的或与合同有关的争议。如果协商未果,合同中又无仲裁条款约定或争议发生后未就仲裁达成协议的,可将争议提交有管辖权的人民法院解决。

Analysis: In this example, "shall" is not a symbol of future tense. It means "must".

Because after a dispute arises, it should be negotiated first, so an obligatory "shall" is adopted. If it cannot be settled through negotiation, as the rights of the parties, an optional "may" is used.

(2) ST: The quality and prices of the commodities to be exchanged between the ex-importers in the two countries shall be acceptable to both sides.

TT: 货物的质量和价格必须使进出口双方都能接受。

Analysis: In a contract, "shall" is generally used to express legally enforceable obligations. If it fails to perform, it shall be deemed as a breach of contract and constitute some kind of liability for compensation. Therefore, in the translation, "shall" is usually translated into "应该". Of course, sometimes it is not translated.

(3) ST: The board meeting shall be convened and presided over by the Chairman. Should the chairman be absent, the vice-Chairman shall, in principle, convene and preside over the board meeting.

TT: 董事会会议应由董事长召集、主持;若董事长缺席,原则上应由副董事长召集、主持。

(4) ST: The formation of this contract, its validity, interpretation, execution and settlement of the disputes shall be governed by related laws of the People's Republic of China.

TT: 本合同的订立、效力、解释、履行和争议的解决均受中华人民共和国法律的管辖。

Analysis: In this sentence, "shall" also has the obligatory meaning, but it is omitted in translation.

(5) ST: By the methods of semantic interpretation, systematic interpretation, interpretation in accordance with the intention of legislator and the interpretation of comparative law, the beneficiary's right to performance may and should be affirmed in the Contract Law.

TT: 通过语义解释、系统解释、立法者解释和比较法解释等方法,合同法可以也应当确认受益人的履行权。

(6) ST: What responsibility should labor contract one party or bilateral breach of contract assume?

TT: 劳动合同一方或双方违反合同应承担什么责任?

Analysis: In example (5) and (6), "should" is translated as "应(应该)". It is used to express expectations, suggestions, or instructional requirements.

5.3.6 Translation of juxtaposition of synonyms

Juxtaposition of synonyms are often used to eliminate the possible ambiguity caused by the polysemy of a word in the contract, so the translator should ensure that the translation corresponds to the original text as much as possible to achieve accuracy, preciseness, standardization and smoothness. For example:

(1) ST: This agreement is made and entered into by and between the parties concerned on September 15, 2020 in Beijing, China on the basis of equality and mutual benefit to

Chapter Five Business English Translation

develop business on <u>terms and conditions</u> mutually agreed upon as follow.

TT：本协议于2020年9月15日在中国北京由有关<u>双方</u>在平等互利基础上<u>达成</u>，根据双方约定的<u>条款</u>开展业务。

Analysis：In this example，"made and entered into" is translated into "达成"，"by and between the parties" is translated into "双方"，and "terms and conditions" is rendered into "条款". Although in English，a parallel synonym is used，in translation only one Chinese word is adopted，because a word for word translation may sound wordy.

However，in some cases，both synonyms are translated as that in example (2) and (3) while in most cases，repetition of the synonyms should be avoided.

(2) ST：Risk of <u>injury or damage</u> exists during emergency operation.

TT：在执行紧急操作期间有造成<u>伤害或损害</u>的危险。

(3) ST：Article 23 upon the <u>expiration or termination</u> in advance of the term of a contractual joint venture, its assets, <u>claims and debts</u> shall be liquidated according to legal procedures.

TT：第二十三条合作企业<u>期满</u>或者提前<u>终止</u>时，应当依照法定程序对资产和<u>债权、债务</u>进行清算。

(4) ST：All <u>terms and conditions</u> will be the same as those in your previous contract number C80065.

TT：所有条款与我们过去签的第C80065号合同规定的各项<u>条款</u>相同。

(5) ST：The Chinese Government shall protect the lawful <u>rights and interests</u> of aliens on Chinese territory.

TT：中国政府保护在中国境内的外国人的合法<u>权益</u>。

(6) ST：In order to specify the <u>duties and responsibilities</u>, legitimate rights and interests of both Parties, Party A and Party B both agree to the provisions herein set forth.

TT：为明确双方<u>权利义务</u>，保护当事人双方的合法权益，特订立如下条款。

(7) ST：Any unauthorized assignment or transfer shall be <u>null and void</u>.

TT：任何未经授权的分配或转让均<u>无效</u>。

(8) ST：The contract becomes <u>null and void</u> when these documents are surrendered.

TT：当这些文件被放弃时合同变得<u>无效</u>。

(9) ST：The letter of guarantee in the contract before the expiry of the warranty in full <u>force and effect</u>.

TT：本保证函在本合同规定的质保期满前完全<u>有效</u>。

(10) ST：The assets will be delivered <u>free and clear of</u> any liens and encumbrances.

TT：资产交付应<u>无</u>任何留置权和产权负担。

(11) ST：The Shareholder's Loan remains due and outstanding to the Vendor, <u>free and clear of</u> any right of off-setting, counterclaims, subordination, encumbrance or other restriction of whatever nature.

TT：未偿清的股东贷款必须支付给买方。股东的贷款<u>不带</u>任何抵销权、反索赔权、附属权、债务权或其他任何性质的<u>约束</u>。

(12) ST: The parties shall, in accordance with the law, have the right to voluntarily conclude and enter into a contract. No unit or individual shall illegally interfere.

TT：当事人依法享有自愿订立合同的权利,任何单位和个人不得干预。

5.3.7　Translation of long complex sentences

Generally speaking, long complex sentences are often used in political articles, scientific papers, archives and bureaucratic papers to express complicated ideas, exquisite sentiments and describe details precisely (Lian, 1993: 74).

This is also the case in contracts which are signed to define both parties' rights and obligations. The terms and conditions specified in the contract have to be defined as clearly and undebatably as possible in order to avoid possibility of disputes, so contract language, for the sake of preciseness, is often characterized by complex sentences by the use of abundant prepositional phrases, adjective phrases, adverbials, attributive clauses etc. Information loss is more likely to occur in the translation of such long complex sentences, so translators must be very careful to guarantee the completeness of the information. For example:

(1) ST: Vetco has used and shall use in performing all the SERVICES and its obligations under this CONTRACT such level of skill, care and diligence so as to ensure that services carried out by the Vetco and all testing performance supplied by the Vetco pursuant to the Contract are of the quality and are sufficient, correct and appropriate to suit SINOPEC's purposes as indicated at Appendix A or as may be reasonably inferred from the Contract.

TT：在提供无损检验服务、履行合同义务的过程当中,Vetco 必须达到相应技术水平,认真细致地工作,确保提供优质的服务,保质保量地完成合同规定的检验工作,达到附件 A 里中石化集团提出的要求,或者满足合同中的合理要求。

Analysis: This article is specifying Party A's quality requirements on testing services. Phrases such as "under this Contract", "pursuant to the Contract", "or as may be reasonably inferred from the Contract" are all modifiers of the key words "services" and "obligations". These modifications must be carefully included in the translation. In addition, division method is used in this translation because English compact sentences is often divided into Chinese diffusive sentences to conform to Chinese expression habit.

(2) ST: SUBCONTRACTOR acknowledges that it has thoroughly investigated, or has had the opportunity to do so, and satisfied itself as to all general and local conditions affecting the WORK, including, but not limited to: transportation and access to the WORK Site, including the availability and conditions of roads; topography and ground surface conditions at the WORK Site, including the nature and quantity of surface and subsurface conditions, materials or obstacles to be encountered to the extent such conditions are not latent or concealed; disposal, handling and storage of materials; availability and quality of labour, water and electric power, climatic conditions, tides and ground water; and

equipment, machinery and materials required by SUBCONTRACTOR prior to and during performance of the WORK.

TT：分包商确认其已经对与工程相关的所有情况以及当地条件做过调查了解（或曾有机会做好此类调查），并对此表示满意。其中包括：进出场道路交通，包括有无道路以及道路状况；工程现场地形以及地表条件，包括地表性质、地表以下的情况、对施工中可能遇到的障碍物清楚明了；材料的处置、搬运与存放；劳动力的供应与素质，水电供应，气候条件，潮汐与地表水；分包商在施工之前以及施工期间所需要的设备、机械和材料。

Analysis: In translation of this long sentence, the completeness of information has to be guaranteed. To achieve this purpose, a structural analysis is very necessary. This long contract article includes a very long objective complement from "including, but not limited to ..." until the very end of the whole sentence. This complement is a long list of items, which can be identified as several categories: transportation, ground conditions, local climate, local supply of manpower and required materials, etc. Each item is then further specified. After the analysis, the meaning of the sentence becomes clear. Then it should be rendered according to Chinese way of expression by division and reorganization and make sure no information has been omitted.

(3) ST: CTOR selects the compensation method described in Paragraph 2.2.1 of the "Attachment V: Subcontract Price and Payment Provisions" as a basis of compensation, subcontractor shall provide contractor, along with the Change Order Price Proposal, a sufficiently detailed breakdown of the proposed Change Order Price along with copies of all related Vendor/Subcontractor quotations for the materials/equipment added or any amount of discount or rebate subcontractor would receive from Vendor(s)/Subcontractor(s), directly or indirectly, for the said materials/equipment and the cost to be ultimately incurred by subcontractor, directly or indirectly, after all direct and indirect discounts and/or rebates to subcontractor.

TT：如果承包商选择附件五"分包合同价格与付款规定"第2.2.1条所规定的补偿方法作为补偿的依据，分包商应随"变更单报价"一起，向承包商提供详细的变更单报价分解、相关供货商/分包商对所增材料/设备的报价、分包商可直接或间接从供货商/分包商处就所增材料/设备所获得的折扣以及分包商在扣除此类直接或间接折扣后所实际承担的最终成本。

Analysis: This is a very long complex sentences which is composed of a protasis and a main clause with five paralleled objects combined by such connecters as "along with", "and", "or". The modifier "directly or indirectly" is used as many as three times to make the idea clearly expressed. First, the translator should analyze the components of the sentence, identify the relationship between the main clause and its modifiers to have a complete understanding of the sentence, then organize the ideas in line with Chinese expressions to make the version smooth and idiomatic.

(4) ST: If a Party breaches any of the representations or warranties given by it in Articles 18.1 or repeated in 18.2, then in addition to any other remedies available to the other Party under this contract or under Applicable Laws, it shall indemnify and keep

indemnified the other Party and the company against any losses, damages, costs, expenses, liabilities and claims that such Party or the Company may suffer as a result of such breach.

TT：如果一方违反任何其根据第 18.1 条或 18.2 条所作的陈述及担保或重述，则另一方除根据本合同或相关法律寻求任何可能的救济之外，违约方应当赔偿另一方或合营公司因此而招致的任何损失、损害、费用、开支、责任或索赔。

（5）ST：The participants in the Joint Venture shall commence discussion with regard to the extension of the period of existence of the Venture and in the event of their agreeing upon such extension, they shall record such agreement in a written document signed by all of them not later than three years prior to the expiry of the current period.

TT：就本合资企业的存续时限的延期问题，各方应进行讨论；一旦各方就此达成一致，应形成书面协议，由各方在本合同期限到期之前的三年内签字生效。

From the above examples, we can see that the methods used in long complex sentences translation is division and reorganization. The principle is complete in information, smooth and understandable in expression.

5.3.8 Translation of passive sentences

In contracts, passive voice is quite commonly used in that it makes the description more objective, and the orders less harsh. However, In Chinese, passive voice is seldom used. Therefore, in E-C translation, we should pay attention to use appropriate methods to translate the passive sentences. For example:

（1）ST：FCC shall notify to contractor, prior to start site works, the name of the person designated as HSE supervisor, whose presence <u>is required</u> on site anytime, who will be responsible for managing and applying FCC Construction HSE Plan. The number of Safety inspectors and/or supervisors to support HSE supervisor/HSE Manager <u>will be specified</u> in the Construction HSE Plan.

TT：在现场开工前，FCC 必须向承包商通报其指定的安全监督员姓名。在现场施工过程中，FCC 的安全监督员<u>必须</u>全天候盯着工地，并负责管理和实施 FCC 的安全施工计划。该计划<u>还必须明确</u> HSE 经理下面有几名监督员，每名监督员下面有几名安全检查员。

Analysis：In the above sentence the verbs "require", and "specify" are both in passive voice. But in the target text these verbs are changed into active voice as is underlined.

Similarly, in the following examples, passive structures are all transformed into active structures in the translation.

（2）ST：Assembly of steel structure components <u>shall be performed</u> at ground level as far as possible, according to structure configuration and lifting equipment capacity.

TT：钢结构的组装要综合考虑结构的外形构造和吊装设备的吊装能力，尽可能在地面<u>进行</u>。

（3）ST：Care should <u>be taken</u> in use, transport and handling of the tool. Falling or hitting against hard objects <u>is strictly prohibited</u>.

TT：仪器<u>要求</u>在使用、运输过程中轻拿轻放，<u>严禁</u>摔打碰撞和敲击，以免造成仪器意外损坏。

(4) ST: Excavation edges or slopes <u>shall be protected</u> by markers or portable barricades. In the event of extremely hazardous edges, in busy and fall areas, use of rigid guardrails is <u>preferred</u>.

TT: 开挖边缘或斜坡<u>必须</u>用警戒线或可移动路障<u>围住</u>。在极度危险的边缘,在人多、易发生坠落区域,<u>建议</u>使用硬性护栏。

(5) ST: The tool should <u>be kept away from</u> magnetic field. Contact or storage with highly magnetic substance must <u>be avoided</u>.

TT: 仪器<u>应远离磁场</u>,<u>避免</u>与强磁物质接触和存放。

(6) ST: If not accomplished before the effective date of this subcontract, within seven days thereafter, subcontractor shall submit to contractor representative an organization chart for the work. Key personnel as designated in the chart <u>shall be assigned</u> to the work and <u>shall not be removed or reassigned</u> without CONTRACTOR prior written permission.

TT: 如果在本分包合同生效日期之前未能完成,则分包商应在本分包合同生效之日后七 (7) 天内向承包商代表提交项目"人员组织机构图"。其中所指定的关键人员要<u>分派到</u>工作地,而且在未征得承包商书面许可的情况下,<u>不得擅自撤出项目或重新指定</u>。

(7) ST: It is mandatory for all construction and erection employees to attend the Safety Induction Session. No employee <u>shall be permitted</u> to work on site or allowed access to the site without first attending the Induction Session.

TT: 所有的施工、安装员工必须参加施工入门安全培训,没有参加安全培训的员工<u>禁止</u>入场。

(8) ST: This Contract <u>is made out</u> in two originals, each copy written in Chinese and English languages, both texts being equally valid. In case of any divergence of interpretation, the Chinese text shall prevail.

TT: 本合同正文一式两份,分别以中文和英文书写,两种文本具有同等效力。若对其解释产生异议,则以中文文本为准。

Analysis: The verb "made out" is omitted in this translation.

5.4 Business Letter Translation

Business correspondence runs through all international business communication activities. As far as the content of letter is concerned, it involves all aspects of international business affairs, including business relationship establishment letter, inquiry letter, review letter, sales letter, order letter, reminder letter of credit, invitation letter, complaint letter, etc. With the development of Internet technology, business English e-letters have become the leading way of international business communication. It is an integral part of international business activities and plays an important role in international business communication.

As far as the communicative style of business English letters is concerned, it belongs to formal official document writing. It has objective, solemn, dignified and rigorous style. The features can be summarized as seven Cs, namely, Completeness, Concreteness, Clearness, Conciseness, Courtesy, Consideration and Correctness (Ren, 2010). This is also the principle in business letter translation.

5.4.1 Correctness

The figures, date and other important information in Business English correspondence must be translated accurately as they often involve the right, the duties and the interest of both sides. Inaccurate translation may bring misunderstanding, even dispute. For example:

(1) ST: The vendor shall deliver the goods to the vendee by July 5.

TT 1:卖方须在7月5日前将货交给买方。

TT 2:卖方须在7月6日前将货交给买方。

Analysis: The first translation is inaccurate and misleading which may cause dispute. The second is accurate. Because in English if the written date is included, the preposition "by" is used; If the written date is not included, that is, until the day before the written date, the preposition "before" is used.

(2) ST: We enclose our Shipping Instructions Form and shall be glad if you will fill this in and return it to us, together with a copy of the invoice for Customs Clearance abroad.

TT 1:随函附寄装船指示单,请填妥后寄回。并附发票一份,供国外结算用。

TT 2:随函附寄装船指示单,请填妥后寄回。并附发票一份,供国外通关用。

Analysis: The first translation is inaccurate because it mistranslated the phrase "Customs Clearance" as "国外结算". Actually, " Customs Clearance" here means "国外通关", so the second translation is accurate.

(3) ST: I apologized for not settling the accountant sooner, but because of the unfortunate disease of Mrs. Lund, our accountant, we are not able to settle any of our outstanding balance.

TT 1:我们没有尽快结清账目,对此我深表歉意。由于我们的会计伦德夫人不幸患病,我们目前无法结清大量余额。

TT 2:我们没有尽快结清账目,对此我深表歉意。由于我们的会计伦德夫人不幸患病,我们目前无法结清未清余额。

Analysis: The first translation is inaccurate because it mistranslated the word "outstanding" as "大量". However, "outstanding" here means "未支付的", so the second translation is accurate.

5.4.2 Courtesy

Courtesy not only can promote friendship but also strengthen and establish trade relationships. Courtesy is not just a greeting. It skillfully expresses the sincere friendship, genuine thanks, good manners, considerate understanding and heartfelt respect. In translation, the polite tone should be rendered. For example:

(1) ST: This corporation is specialized in handing the imports and exports business in electronic products and wishes to enter into business relations with <u>you</u>.

TT：我公司经营电子产品的进出口业务，希望与<u>贵方</u>建立商务关系。

(2) ST: We will definitely be put into more a <u>favorable situation</u> if <u>you</u> are willing to pass your order to us in large quantities.

TT：如果<u>贵方</u>乐意给本公司下大量的订单，本公司必将<u>受惠无穷</u>。

(3) ST: Your large order will be appreciated by us.

TT：请<u>惠赐</u>大量订单。

(4) ST: We will take <u>your</u> requirement into consideration and a discount will be expected if your order is large.

TT：我方对于<u>贵方</u>的要求将予以考虑，如果贵方的订货足够多，我们将提供优惠的价格。

5.4.3 Conciseness

Conciseness is one of the "7C principle" (completeness, concreteness, correctness, conciseness, clearness, courtesy, conscientiousness) of business letters, it means using the least possible words to express the meaning clearly. For example:

(1) ST: Your early reply will be highly appreciated.

TT：静候佳音。

(2) ST: Please find enclosed the check for 1,000,000 dollars and inform us the receipt.

TT：随信附上 100 万美元的支票，收到支票后请通知写信人。

(3) ST: Please reply by fax immediately if you will allow us to delay the shipment until April 21.

TT：如果同意我方将交货时间延期至四月二十一日，请速电复。

However, compared with contracts, interactive letters between different parties are less important. Firstly, one letter is usually concerning one small issue. The information load is smaller. Secondly, unlike contracts, which are constantly referred to during the whole work, most letters are only for temporary use.

But letters have their own important characteristics. Firstly, letters are directly related to work activities, though each letter is usually related to a small issue. Secondly, most letters are instant. The information from work site has to be conveyed to the people concerned instantly. Delay in translation will make the information outdated and even bring about serious consequences. Therefore, instantaneousness should be the first principle in translation of letters. Thirdly, letters are in huge numbers. Letters average over a dozen every day at the peak time of the project. Some letters may be as long as 10 pages. The translation workload is formidable. As a matter of fact, a translator's written translating time is mostly engaged in translation of letters.

The Skopostheorie gives us valuable and practical guidance in letter translation. As Vermeer points out, source text is not the dominating factor in deciding translation principles, but translation purpose is. Source text is just an offer of information from which the translator selects useful and important information in translation, so in letter translation, it is unnecessary to translate literally from the beginning to the end. A practical strategy is to look through the letters for important information and reorganize the key information in a target text, while the redundant part should be omitted in order to improve translation efficiency.

Example 1

  Our Ref. No: MAM/951/07

  Date: 18. 11. 2007

  To: The Fourth Construction Company of SINOPEC.

  Attn: Wang Yongsheng (Vice Chief Engineer)

  Sub: Quotation for Hire of Scaffolders

  Dear Sir,

With reference to the above subject and personal meeting regarding the hire of manpower, we are very interested to supply skilled personal for your project. As per our candidate we would like to quote our offer. Please find below is our best offer.

Sl #.	Category	Rate/ Hour SR.
1	Scaffolders	17/—

  Terms and Conditions:

  Food, Accommodation & Transportation: Scope of The Fourth Construction Company.

  Minimum working hours: 10 hours per day, 6 days in a week and 26 days in a month.

  More than 10 hours & Fridays will be counted as Overtime.

  Employee standby hours should be given.

  Above Rate is Applicable for Overtime also.

  Emergency Medical (First Aid): Scope of The Fourth Construction Company.

  Salary, Gosi & Medical & other documents: scope of Muneer Abbas Al Musahhar cont. Est.

  Timesheet should reach to our office on or before 5th of every following month.

  Payment: 15 days effective from the submission of our Original Invoice.

  Hoping that above quotation is made good and hoping to get your positive response & your valuable Purchase Order.

  We are assuring our best services at all times.

  Thanks & Best Regards,

  For M/S. MUNEER ABBAS AL MUSAHHAR CONT. EST.

       Ismail (050 – 5945573)

       General Manager.

  This is a quotation letter from a human resource establishment to SINOPEC as a response to SINOPEC letter of inquiry. As a quotation, nothing but the unit rate and the terms is the key information. As for the heading of the letter and the formula, no one cares

Chapter Five Business English Translation

much about them. Furthermore, since the terms and conditions are the same as that stipulated in the contract, it is unnecessary to translate them, either. Therefore, this quotation letter can be translated as:

Muneer Abbas 人力资源公司报价：脚手架工单价为 17 里亚尔/小时。用人条款与以前的报价相同。

Example 2

December 12, 2007
L-TRG-FCCSINOPEC-656
To: Branch of the fourth construction company of SINOPEC
Attn: Mr. Wang Yongsheng—project manager
Project: Hawiyah Gas Plant expansion Project
Subject: Work progress
...
Dear Sir,

Regarding the subject mentioned above, TRG informs SINOPEC that the actual construction progress under your scope of work is causing a deviation close to the 12% of the total project schedule.

Below you will find a summary of the areas of concern according to the reported progress, our suggested guidelines, and the most relevant targets of the next coming weeks, in order for you to take immediate actions to revert the underperforming actual progress trend.

<u>Piping prefabrication</u>

Prefabrication along with piping/supports installation is accountable for 85% of the deviation in your scope of work.

Up to now, week after week, we have been requesting to prefabricate at least 12000 ID according to the plan, but no more than a little above 9000 ID have been recently obtained from your shop.

Several issues are impacting the referred targets:

Automatic welding machine are not available 100% of the time mainly because of constant failures of the overhead cranes in the shop and there is not availability of an alternate suitable resource for hauling of the required materials.

Lack of welders and pipe fitters. Even though you reported to have 114 welders, the effective workforce do not exceed 48 at the shop.

Inexistent coordination, planning and supervision makes your production very unproductive and without the proper focus on your installation needs.

Additionally to the mentioned issues, the poor performance of your equipment for blasting and painting makes the real production of your shop well below any industry standard and cause of the big delay and impact in the progress.

We don't want to leave outside our comments on the huge and growing backlog of the NDT as an additional source of attention and needed action from SINOPEC to avoid welding quality problems in the near future.

The actual requirements of the project demand from SINOPEC to put your attention and resources to resolve the mentioned items right away. These issues have been indicated to your in several opportunities. The figures of your progress do not show up to now a satisfactory result from your side.

TRG has targeted for SINOPEC for this week and the coming one a production of 15000 ID per week as a means to correct the actual deviation.

Piping erection

Some of the causes affecting your progress in this subject are the same as the prefabrication but scaled to worse.

Piping erection is a non-organized activity that is reflected in the weekly and cumulative progress. Over the last month you have not been able to reach 2000 ID of total welding in the pipe racks. Several reasons are behind:

Lack of welders and pipe fitters. We have not seen more than a total of 10 welders in GT6 and TOX.

None of your people assigned at the piping erection areas are aware of the erection plans and work priorities, as well.

We have been advising SINOPEC well in advance to get organized for the coming week. Actually several pipe rack are available for piping erection but no action have been seen yet.

Again, lack of planning, enough qualified supervision, resources as welders and pipe fitters are the main reasons of the extremely poor performance. Those are causes of the low progress and quality problems of SINOPEC.

TRG has targeted and request SINOPEC to comply with the completion of the installation and welding of the pipes in the TOX, GT6 main, GT6 East, GT5 main, launcher, and inlet area pipe racks by the end of Dec. 2007.

For your reminder, TRG wants to make you aware, again, that you actually have at your disposition a total of 193000 ID for welding and demands from you immediate actions and results as it was mentioned above.

Equipment

Since the starting of the preparation and erection activities regarding equipment we have been letting you know that not enough resources and planning has been allocated from you for the expected normal development of such works. Lack of cranes, on time erection plans, unavailability of erection accessories have been among the main causes. Even though some of them have finally addressed by you, still some others remain present, such as panning and supervision. Tools are also of concern.

Activities move slowly and once the equipment is put in its foundation or erected no more attention is dedicated, as if took out of your priorities, without given the proper continuity to finalize the work.

TRG have not seen any alignment procedures, grouting activities or hydrotest protocols, where applied, submitted up to date.

Chapter Five Business English Translation

TRG requests SINOPEC to take immediate actions to correct the mentioned deficiencies and give the proper attention and resources in order to avoid more delays and bottlenecks in the near future.

For the present week and the coming one TRG requests SINOPEC to comply at least with the following targets:

Installation of SWS C-002C, GT5 D-511A/B, GT6 D-601A/B, D-608, D-627, DD5 D564, D565, utility equipments E-180, G-180A/B, sulfur condensers E-411, 412, 413, 414; complete installation of E-058, E-059, E-503, including motors and accessories for each of them. Complete the installation of the motors and accessories for E-601, E-603, E-501. Align and put grouting of all the equipment already installed.

Tie-ins

Several meetings have been held regarding the organizational and material resources for accomplishing the critical activities of the project in a safe, well planned and coordinated way. Up to now, TRG has not seen any improvement at all and, instead, the situation is getting worse.

Lack of tools, equipment, planning, supervision, and craftsmanship have been the signature of SINOPEC in the few tie-ins completed up to now.

TRG requests, one more time to SINOPEC, to put in place a dedicated organization with a dedicated person as head of it, with all the resources, before the end of this month to mirror TRG organization for coordination, planning and execution.

TRG expects SINOPEC understand the importance that for Acamco has the completion of the tie-ins safely and on time, because of operational and commercial reasons and request SINOPEC to strictly follow the schedule provided to you.

Electrical and Instrument

Electrical and instrument activities needs also to be provided with more coordination and planning resources. The targets mentioned below will allow SINOPEC to focus his attention and gain additional progress while complying with very important targets.

Electrical

As part of the targets for the actual and next week TRG is setting for SINOPEC the following targets:

To complete cable trays and cable installation in GT6 pipe rack up to E601 and E603.

Additionally to complete cable trays installation for IC1 and IC2 substations, as well as the cable trays in DD5 pipe rack to substation DD2.

Complete conduits and cabling inside SS DD2 and cable trays.

PIB 4 is a high priority target and all remaining activities should be completed before the end of this month.

Instrument

TRG requests SINOPEC to complete all pending items in the PIB 4 building and start the cabinets installation in the next two weeks.

As a final recommendation, TRG sincerely expects that SINOPEC take actions over the mentioned issues causing the major delay in the project and put in place corrective measures to substantially improve the progress.

Our targets are considered mandatory for SINOPEC to comply with scheduled activities for the period.

TRG will answer and provide any needed information that would be considered of your help, as per your request. TRG will also be monitoring the expected daily progress toward the targets, feeding you back permanently with directions and coordination as considered necessary by us.

Best regards!

Site manager: Jose Sola Martinez

(For space reason, the attachments to this letter are omitted from this citing. By author)

This is a letter from TRG, the main contractor, to SINOPEC, the subcontractor, concerning the work progress of the project. Plus the heading and attachments, the letter is more than 3 pages long. It would have taken hours to translate it word-for-word, whereas the text user may finish reading the translation fruit in a minute, as many parts of the letter provide no valuable information at all.

The purpose of the original letter is to inform SINOPEC of the delay in work progress, further analyze the causes of the delay and then set mandatory targets for the next two weeks. The intention of the author is to shake off their responsibility for the delay of the work. From the view of SINOPEC, the work delay is mostly due to the lack of materials, which is within the scope of TRG, instead of the reasons that TRG argues. TRG holds no water in their argument that the delay is mainly attributed to SINOPEC, so the function of the target text is not in complete accordance with the original. What a translator should do is to represent the arguments that TRG makes. As to the creditability, it is up to SINOPEC PMT (project management team) to decide.

Project letters, as a kind of practical writing, care little about their literary value, so it is unnecessary to keep the style of the original letter. The tone and person of the original letter can also be changed. The minor details can be omitted. There is very little chance that the writer should complain about the translator's violation of his authorship. Therefore, the translator should organize the target text for the sole purpose of information communication. The following is the translation of the over-10-page long letter.

主题：工程进度问题（TRG 第 656 号来信）

SINOPEC 承包范围内的工程进度比计划慢了将近 12%。对此，TRG 作了如下的分区总结，提出了建议，并设定接下来两周的工作目标。

管道预制

误工的 85% 的原因是由于管道预制、配管/管支架安装。我们设定的预制目标是每周 12000 ID，而贵方的实际预制仅仅达到每周 9000 ID。TRG 认为误工原因如下：

(1) 缺自动焊机，天车性能不佳，故障频繁；

(2) 缺焊工、管工；

(3)缺乏工作的协调、计划和监管；
(4)喷砂、喷漆设备性能不佳；
(5)无损检验的效率跟不上；
本周及下周的预制新目标为每周 15000 ID。

管道安装
管道预制进度缓慢,上个月贵方的管道安装才不到每周 2000 ID。TRG 认为原因是施工组织不力,计划不周,监督不力；缺乏焊工、管工。
TRG 要求 SINOPEC 在 2007 年 12 月底之前完成下列区域的管道安装：热氧化区(TOX)、GT6 主管廊及东管廊、GT5 主管廊、发射装置区、入口区管廊。

设备
我们多次提醒,贵方计划不够周详,资源调配不力,吊车不足,安装计划没有及时制订,安装辅件不足,工具问题也必须注意。
SINOPEC 至今仍没有提交设备找正、基础灌浆以及试压方案。
本周及下周设备安装的目标是（按照设备代号）：SWS C－002C,GT5 D－511A/B,GT6 D－601A/B,D－608,D－627,DD5 D564,D565,公用设备 E－180,G－180A/B,硫磺冷凝器 E－411,412,413,414;E－058,E－059,E－503,包括上述设备的电机和配件的安装；还有 E－601,E－603,E－501 的电机和附件的安装。为所有安装完毕的设备找正、灌浆。

"太印"
迄今为止,太印完成的数量屈指可数,TRG 认为误工原因是缺乏工具、设备、计划监管以及技工。
业主基于运营和商业上的考虑,要求我们安全、及时地完成太印,TRG 希望 SINOPEC 积极配合,务必严格按照计划施工。

电仪
本周及下周电气的目标是：
(1)完成 GT6 的管廊上到 E601 和 E603 的电缆桥架和电缆安装；
(2)完成 IC1 和 IC2 变电站的电缆桥架安装,以及 DD5 管廊到 DD2 变电站的电缆桥架安装；
(3)完成 SS、DD2 的导管和电缆以及电缆桥架安装；
(4)注意 PIB4 是当前的优先目标,所有尾项必须在本月末完成；
仪表的目标是：SINOPEC 必须在两周内完成 PIB 4 内的所有未完成的施工,并开始控制室的安装。

This target text is shortened into a one-page text with the key information maintained. Some paragraphs are deleted as a whole since they provide no significant information at all. It should be noted that as to the analysis of the delay of the work, the translator highlights the agent of the analysis, that is, TRG, in order to emphasize that the analysis might be subjective and partial.

While applying the strategy of "select and translate" and "edit and translate" into the translating of interactive letters, one basic principle has to be observed. The translator has to make good judgment in processing the information on the base of a thorough understanding of the source text so that no important information is skipped and the redundant parts removed.

Chapter Six C-E Translation of Fine Art Commentary

With the continuous improvement of China's international status and the growth of its economic and military strength, China's influence on world affairs is becoming tremendous. Its extensive culture and long history deeply attracted the attention of people from all walks of life at home and abroad. The fine art works is a window to introduce our history, culture and economic development to the world. It is the way through which the painters express their ideas, depict people's life, reflect the spirit of a nation and convey the values and moral of a country.

In recent years, international exchange in art circles has been very active. Artists of different art categories in China have actively participated in the overseas art exhibitions, auctions, academic exchanges and international competitions. Therefore, the translation of the promotional commentaries plays a very important role in international communication in art fields and it is an effective way to tell the Chinese story to the world. It helps people in other countries to understand China's culture, history, development and its brand-new appearance.

As a genre of writing, fine art commentary is the comment, explanation or evaluation of visual art through describing, analyzing, interpreting the specific works of art to help viewers perceive, interpret, and appreciate art works. It is an integral part of art exhibitions or art albums, which aims to promote the art works and stir response from the viewers.

This chapter will take the translation of a series of commentaries on Professor Wang Haili's oil paintings exhibited in Chinese People's Revolutionary Military Museum as a case analysis.

"China Dream, Strong Army Dream"—Exhibition of Wang Haili's paintings was held to commemorate the 70th anniversary of the victory of the Chinese people's anti-Japanese War and the World Anti-fascist War as well as the 88th anniversary of the founding of the People's Liberation Army. Mr. Wang Haili is a professor in Xi'an Academy of Fine Arts. He is famous for revolutionary-themed paintings. In the exhibition, more than 70 pieces of Wang Haili's oil painting were displayed. The theme of the exhibition is remembering historical lessons, having firm faith in the party, bearing in mind the mission to realize China dream and strong army dream. The theme of Professor Wang's oil paintings were mainly picked up from historical stories and revolutionary events to reveal the heroic spirit of

Chapter Six C-E Translation of Fine Art Commentary

Chinese nation in fighting against enemy invasion throughout thousands of years' history. The paintings highlight the mainstay function of the Communist Party in the Anti-Japanese War and the contributions made by the army.

The commentaries introduce the theme, contents and artistic skills of professor Wang's paintings. The main function is to help the audience to understand the paintings and appeal to Chinese people's love to our nation and army, and uplift Chinese people's patriotic spirit.

6.1 Functions of the Target Text

As is mentioned above, the exhibition of Prof. Wang Haili's oil paintings would be held in Chinese People's Revolutionary Military Museum. During the expo, many international leaders and journalists would visit the exhibition. Therefore, an effective and accurate translation would help the foreign audience to understand the theme and artistic value of the paintings. In addition, it is a best way to introduce China's national defense policy, military mission, history, achievements and army modernization to the world so that they can have a real understanding of China's military policy and actions of the Chinese government. The source text is written for Chinese readers, while the TT is intended for foreign readers, so the translator should consider the readers' background knowledge, culture, language expression habit, etc., in translation.

6.2 Linguistic Features of the Source Text

As a special type of text, art commentary has its own features which distinguish itself from general text.

6.2.1 Vivid words and expressions

Art works, just like music, is a universal media of communication, so the content must be expressed through visual perception. In order to precisely convey the picture's content and purport, the critics of the art works usually use vivid expressions such as abundant adjectives, set phrases (Chinese four-character *Chengyu*) to depict the paintings or pictures. In the source text of Wang Haili's oil painting commentary, there are many such descriptions. For example：

(1)……背景虚化处理,简化复杂的战场,用风起云涌、硝烟弥漫渲染战场气氛,烘托主体。虚实相间中营造出英雄战将,金戈铁马,浩荡雄风,无坚不摧,无往不胜的强大震慑力。

(2)《庄严昭告》取材于2012年11月29日。那一天上午,北京风和日丽,长安街车水马龙,天安门广场游人如织……

In the above two examples, set phrases are used to create a vivid picture of the spirit or scene revealed in the painting, which requires great attention in translation.

6.2.2　Culture–specific words and expressions

Since fine art is the reflection of life, it is not just only confined to aesthetics itself, but also covers many other subjects like history, sociology, politics, philosophy, religion, special cultures such as customs and holidays. In the commentary of Professor Wang Haili's oil paintings, there involves many culture-loaded expressions about historical figures, dynasties, important national events, government leaders. For example,"秦始皇""张骞""习近平总书记""邓小平""抗日战争""汉唐雄风""周秦汉唐""戚继光战倭大捷""马踏飞燕""玄奘西行那烂陀""蒋家王朝", etc.

Native speakers may find such expressions easy to understand, while foreigners may have no ideas about Chinese history, tradition, or important national events, so proper methods should be adopted to translate such culture-specific words and phrases to achieve the intended effect of communication.

6.2.3　Topic predominate construction and diffusive sentence structure

Apart from subject-predicate structure sentences in Chinese, there is another type of sentence structure in which the relationship between the word in the subject position and the verb in the predicate position are not actor and actions, but "topic and comment". The topic here refers to something that the speaker brings up to be talked about, namely the theme. The rest of the sentence following the topic is the comment in which the theme is developed, commented, explained or questioned which can be very long and characterized by paratactic structure (Lian, 1993: 66). This type of sentences are composed of several independent clauses which are presented in chronologic order or cause-effect order by using less grammatical devices such as conjunctions, prepositions, relative pronouns, relative adverbs or other connective devices; therefore, the sentences tend to be diffusive, short, loose and most long sentences are composed of both complete sentences and a lot of phrases. For example:

（1）王海力长期以来不抱偏见，打破门派，广采博收，掌握了多种多样的艺术手法，能够得心应手地运用，机动灵活地发挥，随心所欲不拘一格地组合，所以才能创作出许多绚烂多姿、震撼心灵的油画作品。

（2）王海力在几十年学油画、教油画的艺术生涯中，不仅练就了西洋油画的写实造型功力，深入理解了它的美学原理（见《塔什库尔干的喜庆》《藏巴汉子》等），同时作为中国画家，他努力领悟中国艺术美学的写意精神，并且广采博收各种绘画种类的表现方式，他尝试用油画表现中国山水画虚实相间的意境，吸收壁画、宣传画突出主体、多画面组合的时空优势……把中国传统绘画美学的"虚实相生""一以当十""计白当黑""情景交融"等观念和西方现代主义非写实美学理论，与传统油画的写实再现相结合，运用到重大历史题材油画创作中。

In the above two sentences, "王海力" is the topic, the rest of the sentences and clauses being the comment. In these two sentences, complete sentences and phrases mix together according to logic orders without connectives showing the relationship between different parts, so it's often difficult to tell the subject from the predicate, the main clause from the subordinate. Such running sentences are very common in Chinese art commentaries; therefore, they deserve much attention in translation.

6.3 Criteria for Art Text Translation

Broadly speaking, translation standards are universal for all kinds of texts, so the translation of art commentary should also follow the same rules. However, because of the distinguished features of the art commentary, the criterion of translation has its special characteristics.

According to functionalist translation theory, more attention should be paid to the function of the TT and its readers. Therefore, a reader-oriented approach is proved to be the effective way in art commentary translation. In order to achieve the communicative effect, appropriate translation skills must be employed to make the TT smooth, readable, vivid, comprehensive and professional.

6.4 Translation Methods of Fine Art Commentary

Since functional translation is target language biased, which emphasizes more on social effect and function of the target text, communicative translation method is often adopted to cater for the TT culture, making the translation more acceptable to readers. Therefore, when translating the art commentaries of Professor Wang Haili's oil paintings, flexible translation methods such as amplification, omission, division, combination, paraphrasing, and restructuring are adopted to make the translation smooth, accurate, idiomatic and understandable.

6.4.1 Amplification

Amplification, also known as addition, is a strategy used in translation by adding information to TT on the basis of accurate comprehension of the original text. Since English and Chinese are two different languages and each has its own cultures and traditions, some content which is familiar to the ST readers is not necessarily acceptable to TT readers. Therefore, it is necessary for translators to make some adjustments so as to live up to the readers' expectations. Generally, two techniques are employed. One is to explain and supplement something that does not exist in the ST language such as background knowledge and cultural elements. The other is to add connective devices to make the translated version more acceptable.

1. Amplification by adding background information

When names of people, places of historical events, or cultural-loaded words and expressions appear in ST which present difficulties for TT readers who do not share the same background, amplification is often resorted to make the version understandable.

Example 1

ST: 展出的 70 多幅画作, 凸现了中华民族从<u>周秦汉唐</u>以来, 振兴中华、抵御外侮的重大历史事件和民族英雄。从秦始皇统一六国(《一统六合》)、张骞出使<u>西域</u>(《大汉张骞》)到领导中国人民推翻<u>三座大山</u>建立新中国的伟大领袖毛泽东(《数风流人物》)

TT: More than 70 oil paintings displayed highlight the important historical events and national heroes in revitalizing our nation and fighting against invaders <u>from Zhou (1046 B. C.), to Tang Dynasty (907 A. D.)</u>. For example, the painting Unification of the Six States tells the story of Qinshihuang (221 – 207 B. C.), <u>the First Emperor in Chinese history</u>, who united China; *Han Dynasty Zhang Qian*, depicts Zhang Qian's Mission (164 – 114 B. C.) to the Western regions (<u>today's west Asian area</u>). In his painting *Truly Great Men in History*, Chairman Mao Zedong is the main character, who led Chinese people overthrow <u>the oppression of feudalism, imperialism and bureaucrat capitalism</u> and finally established Peoples' Republic of China.

Analysis: In this example, The ST involves historical dynasties like "周秦汉唐", historical figures like "秦始皇","张骞","毛泽东", places like "西域" and historical events like "推翻'三座大山'". All these terms are Chinese culture-specific which present difficulties for TT readers if translated directly without any explanation, so amplification method (the underlined parts in the TT) is used by adding the time of the dynasties and specific explanations of the historical characters, places and events so that the communicative effect can be realized in the TT.

Example 2

ST: 如画毛泽东、习近平, 观众首先要看画得像不像, 只有像才能取得观众的认可。

TT: For example, if Mao Zedong—<u>the founder of PRC</u> or Xi Jinping—<u>the General Secretary</u> of the Central Committee is painted, the audience will firstly see whether the picture is like the real person or not, otherwise it cannot be accepted.

Analysis: When translating the political leaders "Mao Zedong" and "Xi Jiping", we amplified the necessary information (the underlined parts in the TT) so that the readers know who these important figures are and how important they are and why they are depicted in the art works.

2. Amplification by adding necessary connectives

As is analyzed in 3.4.4, Chinese sentences are characterized by paratactic structure, which are often formed by logic order of cause and effect or chronological orders without using many grammatical devices such as relative pronouns, relative adverbs, propositions, conjunctions, vocabulary devices like pronouns, etc., therefore Chinese sentences tends to be diffusive. Unlike Chinese, English tends to be compact because the relationship between each part of the sentence is made clear by using a large number of connectives. So in C-E translation, connective devices, pronouns have to be added in most cases to make the TT readable and idiomatic.

Chapter Six C-E Translation of Fine Art Commentary

Example 1

ST：对于历史而言，也是一样，现当代和我们距离近，人们了解的比较多；古代和我们距离远，人们了解的比较少，创作中画家采取今实古虚的处理。

TT：This also applies to history. The modern and contemporary events are close to us, so people know more about them, while the ancient events are far away from us, so people know less about them; therefore, the painter adopts realistic methods to depict modern events and virtual approach to deal with the ancient events.

Example 2

ST：王海力长期以来不抱偏见，打破门派，广采博收，掌握了多种多样的艺术手法，能够得心应手地运用，机动灵活地发挥，随心所欲不拘一格地组合，所以才能创作出许多绚烂多姿、震撼心灵的油画作品。

TT：Having no prejudices, breaking off the schools, learning extensively, Wang Haili has mastered a wide variety of artistic techniques so he can use them flexibly in his painting through free combination. As a result, he has created many gorgeous and soul-shocking oil paintings.

Analysis：In the above examples, conjunctions and adverbs (the underlined parts) are added to transform the Chinese diffusive sentences into English subject-predicate sentences. After adjusting the sentence structures by such devices, the relationship between different parts of the sentence becomes clearer in the TT.

3. Amplification by adding necessary pronouns

Example 1

ST：领袖人物的创作，采取了多图层重叠的手法，打破景物实际比例，像宣传画似的突出领袖人物。

TT：When he created the image of the great leaders, he adopts the overlapping multi-layer technique to break the actual proportion of the scene and highlight the leaders as that in posters.

Analysis：In Chinese, there are many subject omitting sentences. When they are translated into English, subject must be added to make the sentence complete and idiomatic. That's why pronoun "he" is added in this translation.

Example 2

ST：王海力 2006 年作为访问学者赴巴黎高等美术学院学习，在欧洲参观了近百个博物馆画廊。2010 年又赴俄罗斯列宾美术学院考察学习，写生创作了许多俄罗斯风景。

TT：In 2006, Mr. Wang studied at Ecole Nationale Superieure Des Beaux-Arts as a visiting scholar. During that time, he visited about 100 European museums and galleries. In 2010, Wang studied at Repin Academy of Fine Arts in Russia where he created a number of oil paintings about the landscapes of Russia.

Analysis：This is a typical Chinese topic-prominent sentence. In this type of sentence, once the topic is settled, the logic subjects of the rest sentences which comment and supplement the topic are often omitted. However, the omitted subjects of the commenting sentences should be supplied (the underlined pronouns) in the TT to make it a smooth English sentence.

6.4.2 Omission

Omission, also referred to as deletion, is a skill adopted in translation by deleting some redundant information which carries little meaning to the TT readers due to cultural reasons and aesthetic standards. In C-E translation, some historical figures, name of people or name of small places are often omitted, because if these culture-specific items are kept, it would be difficult for the TT readers to figure out the meaning and message.

Example 1

ST：从秦始皇统一中华(《一统六合》)、张骞出使西域(《大汉张骞》)、唐太宗李世民(《唐王出征》《大唐天可汗》),到表现中国历代战功卓著的将领<u>李牧、蒙恬、霍去病、裴行俭</u>,令十万金兵闻风丧胆的<u>岳飞、戚继光</u>等叱咤风云的英雄气概(《战必胜》《战神白起》《兵出正道王翦》《戚继光战倭大捷》等)……

TT：For example, the painting *Unification of the Six States* tells the story of Qinshihuang (221 – 207 B.C.), the First Emperor in Chinese history, who united China; "*Han Dynasty Zhang Qian*, depicts Zhang Qian's Mission (164 – 114 B.C.) to the Western regions (today's west Asian area). *Tang Emperor on the Battle*, *The King of the Great Tang Empire* describe the heroic deeds of the Tang emperor (598 – 649 A.D.). <u>Many other famous historical figures in different dynasties also become the main characters in his paintings</u>, showing their heroic deeds and patriotic spirits.

Analysis：In the above example, the historical figures like "李牧、蒙恬、霍去病、裴行俭、岳飞、戚继光" are strange to TT readers, so they are generalized into "many other famous historical figures in different dynasties" by omitting the specific names.

Example 2

ST：党的十八大刚闭幕半个月,中共中央总书记习近平和中央政治局常委<u>李克强、张德江、俞正声、刘云山、王岐山、张高丽</u>一同来到国家博物馆,参观大型主题展览《复兴之路》。

TT：Just two weeks after the close of the 18th National Congress, <u>General Secretary of CPC Central Committee</u> Xi Jinping, and <u>other six members</u> of the Standing Committee of the Political Bureau gathered together in the National Museum to visit the grand theme exhibition "Road to Revival".

Analysis：Because some western readers are not familiar with the names of Chinese leaders—李克强、张德江、俞正声、刘云山、王岐山、张高丽, it is unnecessary to translate out their names. Instead, they are generalized as "other six members of the Standing Committee". By this way, the TT can become more comprehensible.

Example 3

ST：《温暖》这幅油画,取材于 2013 年深秋(11 月 3 日),习近平到我国<u>14 个集中连片特困地区</u>之一的武陵山区湘西土家族苗族自治州考察时,在土家族聚居的<u>花垣县十八洞村</u>特困老人施齐文家的情景。

Chapter Six　C-E Translation of Fine Art Commentary

TT: The oil painting *Warmth* was based on an event happened in the late autumn of 2013 (Nov. 3) when General Secretary Xi Jinping visited Shi Qiwen, an extremely poor farmer, during Xi's inspection to one of the poor-stricken mountain village in west Hunan Province.

Analysis: In this example, the name of the small village "花垣县十八洞村" and "14个集中连片" carries little meaning in the TT, so they are omitted for the reason of conciseness.

6.4.3　Division

Division means necessary splitting of a long sentence into several short sentences according to the meaning group. Some Chinese diffusive sentences, with different parts linked only by comma, are very long and complicated. Such sentences have several layers of meaning, so it would be difficult to understand if translated according to the original structure. In this case, they are often divided into several independent sentences so that the translated version would be smooth and understandable.

Example 1

ST: 王海力在几十年学油画、教油画的艺术生涯中,不仅练就了西洋油画的写实造型功力,深入理解了它的美学原理(见《塔什库尔干的喜庆》《藏巴汉子》等),同时作为中国画家,他努力领悟中国艺术美学的写意精神,并且广采博收各种绘画种类的表现方式,他尝试用油画表现中国山水画虚实相间的意境,吸收壁画、宣传画突出主体、多画面组合的时空优势……把中国传统绘画美学的"虚实相生""一以当十""计白当黑""情景交融"等观念和西方现代主义非写实美学理论,与传统油画的写实再现相结合,运用到重大历史题材油画创作中。

TT: During decades of art career of learning and teaching oil painting, Wang Haili not only practiced the realistic modeling skills of western oil painting, but also deeply understood its aesthetic principles (reflected in *Festival of Taxkorgan*, *Tibetan Men*, etc.), but also apprehend the freehand spirit of Chinese aesthetics and adopts all kinds of painting methods. // He tries to express Chinese landscape by absorbing the oil paintings, murals and picture posters to highlight the theme. // When he created paintings about great historical events, he combined the aesthetic ideas of traditional Chinese painting such as "Combination real images with virtual ones", "one to serve as ten", "blank as inked", "Integration of feelings with settings" with the western modernism non-realistic aesthetics theory in his creation.

Example 2

ST: 油画《庄严昭告》和新中国经典油画《开国大典》《黄河颂》《毛主席去安源》《蒋家王朝的覆灭》《父亲》一样,之所以为广大普通老百姓喜爱和牢记,是因为它们有着共同的特质:以艺术形式再现了中华民族历史的重大时刻,是中华民族历史可歌可泣的光辉一页。

TT: Like other classical paintings created after 1949 such as *Founding Ceremony*, *Ode to the Yellow River*, *Chairman Mao Goes to Anyuan*, *Destruction of Chiang Dynasty* and *Father*, the oil painting *Solemn Proclamation* has also won popularity among majority of ordinary people for their common traits. // They represent the important moment of the Chinese history in the form of art and become a glorious page of our nation.

Example 3

ST：画家大胆探索用艺术手法构筑了一个精神与美的世界，他用想象力来营造统摄绘画语境，把具有特定意义的意象符号通过色彩、构图的韵律排布，营造出超意象的质感效果，每一部分都处在一个被发现的位置里，连接着梦想与现实，使油画的意义既能达致完整清晰，又能提供高尚愉悦的感官享受，二者巧妙的结合让作品达到了完美与和谐的意境。

TT：The painter boldly builds a world of spirit and beauty with artistic technique. // He used his imagination to manage the painting context by arranging specific image symbols through the rhythm of color and composition to create a texture effect of super image. // With each component standing out on its own, connecting dreams and reality, the whole picture provides noble and pleasant sensory enjoyment. // The ingenious combination of the two makes the work reach a perfect and harmonious artistic conception.

Analysis：In the above three examples, the original long sentences are divided into two or several English subject-predicate sentences according to the meaning groups so that the meaning of the translated version becomes clearer to the English readers and the communicative effect is achieved effectively.

6.4.4 Combination

Combination means combining two or more simple sentences or clauses into a long English sentence. Some Chinese diffusive sentences are made of several short sentences and phrases without using connectives to show the relationship between different parts. If such sentences are translated rigidly according to the original sentence structure, the translated version would be awkward. Instead, if the loose sentences are combined by using appropriate connectives such as relative adverbs, relative pronouns, conjunctions and prepositions, the logic meaning would be expressed explicitly so that the translation would be coherent and fluent.

Example 1

ST：崇高是人类各民族的英雄们在艰难险阻的斗争中表现的英勇顽强、坚忍不拔、无私无畏的精神意志，成为民族群体伟大的精神旗帜，体现了人类开拓前进、创造历史的本质力量。

TT：Loftness is the spiritual will of heroes of all nations who show their bravery, perseverance, and selfless fearlessness in the hardship and dangerous struggle, and becomes great spiritual symbol of the nation, which reflects the essential power of human beings to forge ahead and create history.

Example 2

ST：王海力跳出写实再现的困扰，充分发挥想象，大刀阔斧地自由挥洒，突出气势、淡化情节，夸张地表现人物精神气质。

TT：Jumping out of the trouble of realistic representation, Wang Haili gives full play to his imagination to express the ethos of the characters exaggeratedly by highlighting the momentum and weakening the plot.

Example 3

ST: 而王海力以及他同时代的一批优秀画家,也以自己的不懈实践,表明了中国油画的发展之路是宽阔的,与时代同步,与人民同心,与自然对话,中国油画一定会走出自己的广阔道路,走向世界。

TT: At the same time, the hard work and achievement by Wang Haili and many other outstanding contemporary painters in China indicate that Chinese oil paintings will have a bright future and can finally go to the world as long as the artists keep pace with the times and care about people's life and nature.

Analysis: In the above examples, connectives such as relative pronoun "which", "who", "that", conjunctions like "and", "as long as", "by" are employed to combine the diffusive Chinese sentences into English compact sentences to explicitly dig out the relationship between different parts of the sentences. After combination, the sentences become more idiomatic for the TT readers.

6.4.5 Paraphrasing

Paraphrasing is an effective way to retrieve the essential information of a language element which has no equivalence in another language. It is often used together with the technique of omission and generalization to distill a Chinese version written in rhetoric language into succinct English. Paraphrasing works well with the translation of titles, culture-loaded expressions, set phrases (Chinese idioms), and rhetoric expressions in art critic text to fulfill the intended function.

1. Paraphrasing titles and subtitles of the paragraphs and text

Titles and subtitles in Chinese articles are often rhetoric, with verbose expressions and antithesis, which is often over-generalized and abstract, so in C - E translation, paraphrase is often adopted to make the abstract expressions concrete and the over-generalized ideas specific based on the full understanding of the whole part.

2. Paraphrasing the titles of the paintings

Titles of the paintings are difficult to translate not only because titles reflect the content of the painting, but also because the culture elements contained and historical events described. The language is refined and the connotation is profound, so paraphrase is an effective skill to tackle the problem.

Example 1

ST: 从秦始皇统一六国(《一统六合》)、张骞出使西域(《大汉张骞》)、唐太宗李世民(《唐王出征》《大唐天可汗》),到现代史上伟大壮烈的抗日战争,领导中国人民推翻三座大山建立新中国的伟大领袖毛泽东(《数风流人物》《铁血抗战铸军魂》《抗战老兵》等)。

TT: For example, the painting *Unification of the Six States* tells the story of Qinshihuang (221 - 207 B. C.), the First Emperor in Chinese history, who united China;

Han Dynasty Zhang Qian, depicts Zhang Qian's Mission (164 – 114 B. C.) to the Western regions (today's west Asian area). *Tang Emperor on the Battle*, *The King of the Great Tang Empire* describes the heroic deeds of the Tang emperor (598 – 649 A. D.). … In his painting *Truly Great Men in History*, Chairman Mao Zedong is the main character, who led Chinese people overthrow the oppression of feudalism, imperialism and bureaucrat capitalism and finally established Peoples' Republic of China. In *Blood Cast Soul Resistance Against Japan* and *Veterans of Anti-Japanese War*, the painter depicts the brave behavior of Chinese people in Anti-Japanese War.

Analysis: Here "《一统六合》" is paraphrased as "*Unification of the Six States*", "《唐王出征》" as "Tang Emperor on the Battle", "《数风流人物》" as "Truly Great Men in History". These versions clearly convey the meaning and message of the paintings and become comprehensible to the TT readers.

Example 2

ST:《一统六合》《战必胜》《出兵正道王翦》《大将白起》《戚继光战倭大捷》等,都采用了主体实、背景虚的构图。

TT: When creating *Unification of the Six States*, *Unconquerable Forces*, *Fighting for Justice led by general Wang Jian*, *God of War—Bai Qi*, *Victory of Qi Jiguang against Japanese*, etc., the painter adopted the composition technique of real subject and virtual background.

Analysis: In this example, "《战必胜》《出兵正道王翦》《大将白起》《戚继光战倭大捷》" are put into *Unconquerable Forces*, *Fighting for Justice by General Wang Jian*, *God of War—Bai Qi*, *Victory of Qi Jiguang against Japanese* respectively, which convey the message and spirit of the paintings vividly and exactly by paraphrasing.

3. Paraphrasing culture-loaded expressions

Example 1

ST:中心位置的那匹马,人们一眼就能看出是著名的出土文物《马踏飞燕》的造型,一下就把我们带到了遥远的西汉时代。

TT: The horse at the center position imitates the famous unearthed *The Running Horse*, which suddenly brings people back to the ancient Western Han Dynasty.

Analysis: In this example, "马踏飞燕" is a classical allusion, which would be difficult for the TT readers to understand if the story is not told. However, it is inappropriate to elaborate on the allusion here, so it is paraphrased as the "The Running Horse" according to the image. This translation is not only informative, but also vivid and concise.

Example 2

ST:《大唐天可汗》是一个平面化的主体中心构图,大胆采用了壁画常用的构图样式,中心人物唐太宗李世民在画面的中心,正面表现帝王之相、九五之尊。

TT: *The King of the Great Tang Empire* is a flat main character-centered composition, boldly adopting the composition style of fresco painting. The main character Li Shimin, the emperor, is painted at the center of the picture with his majesty face to the

Chapter Six C-E Translation of Fine Art Commentary

audience.

Analysis: In this sentence, "帝王之相、九五之尊" is rendered into "the emperor... with his majesty face to the audience", thus the essential information is retrieved of the Chinese rhetoric expression.

4. Paraphrasing the poems and quotations

Example 1

ST: 在《数风流人物》中,写实的肖像以特写突现在画面前方中心,背景是"山舞银蛇,原驰蜡象"的北国风光,色调单纯统一,在这两个图层合并时,放大人物,缩小背景,凸显领袖"欲与天公试比高"的英雄气概!

TT: In *Truly great men in History*, Chairman Mao's image is placed at the front center of the picture, while the background is the Northern landscape of lofty mountains and snow-covered grand plateau. When the two layers combine, the figure is enlarged while the background is reduced to highlight the leader's heroic spirit of "Competing against the God".

Analysis: In the ST, "山舞银蛇,原驰蜡象" and "欲与天公试比高" are sentences extracted from Chairman Mao's poem, which are familiar to Chinese readers, but to the TT readers who has no background knowledge, literal translation would be infeasible, so paraphrasing (the underlined parts) is the best way to deal with poems and classic quotations in informative text.

Example 2

ST: 国家存亡,匹夫有责。他不能沉浸在"浅斟低唱"中虚度年华,而是勇敢地、满怀激情地响应时代召唤,担当起历史使命,把自己的艺术生命融汇到实现中华民族伟大复兴的中国梦的宏伟交响乐之中!

TT: The survival of the nation requests everyone to do his duty. He cannot waste his time by immersing in self-enjoyment but only bravely and passionately responding to the call of the times, assuming the historical mission, putting his artistic life into grand symphony of realizing Chinese dream of great rejuvenation.

Analysis: Chinese tend to use classic sayings and verbiage expressions to express feelings or make comments, but such expressions have no equivalence in English, so paraphrase (the underlined parts) is often resorted to solve the problem.

5. Paraphrasing set phrases (Chinese *Chengyu*)

Set phrases, the four-character Chinese idioms, is also called phrasal idioms or idiomatic expressions whose meaning are fixed and sometimes cannot be inferred from the meanings of the words that makes it up. Set phrases reflect the wisdom of Chinese people, because they are so concise that the four character phrases can express very rich meaning. Since this is the unique feature of Chinese language, and there is no ready-made equivalence in English, paraphrase is often employed in set phrase translation.

Example 1

ST:《庄严昭告》取材于2012年11月29日。那一天上午,北京风和日丽,长安街车水马龙,天安门广场游人如织。

TT：*Solemn Proclamation* is based on a <u>sunny morning</u> on November 29, 2012 when Chang'an Street and Tian'anmen Square <u>was thronged with vehicles and visitors</u>.

Example 2

ST：周边把不同时空场景的几个很小画面点缀在背景上。背景虚化处理,简化复杂的战场,用风起云涌、硝烟弥漫渲染战场气氛,烘托主体。虚实相间中营造出英雄战将<u>金戈铁马</u>,浩荡雄风,<u>无坚不摧</u>,<u>无往不胜</u>的强大震慑力。

TT：At the same time, a few small pictures of different space-time scenes are interspersed in the background, which is virtually treated and simplifies the complexity of the <u>battlefield with the rising storm</u> and <u>smoke of the battlefield</u>, thus highlighting the subject, so the heroes' <u>powerful will</u>, <u>invincible temperament</u> and <u>unconquerable spirit and deterrent</u> are expressed vividly by the interaction of actual and virtual composition.

Example 3

ST：这幅体现总书记心系民瘼温暖之情的作品,无论是在思想的深刻性上,还是在艺术的独创性方面,都堪称<u>出类拔萃</u>,特别值得我们珍视。画名之曰《温暖》,颇有<u>画龙点睛</u>、<u>引人入胜</u>之妙。

TT：This painting which embodies the great concern and warm care of General Secretary Xi's to people is considered as an <u>outstanding masterpiece</u> in both the depth of thought and in the artistic originality, which deserves treasuring. The title "Warmth" can really <u>reflect the theme of the painting</u>, thus <u>becoming very fascinating</u>.

Analysis：With regard to these three examples, the Chinese version is no doubt eloquent, descriptive and impressive. The vivid expressions of the ST are realized by paraphrasing, which would be impossible by a word for word translation. Therefore, paraphrase is the first choice to transmit the implied meaning of set phrases.

6.4.6 Restructuring

Restructuring means necessary or inevitable change or adjustment of the word order or the structure of a sentence of ST to make the version more smooth, readable and acceptable according to the expression habit of the TT readers.

Example 1

ST：习近平总书记指出：只有坚持洋为中用、开拓创新,做到中西合璧、融会贯通,<u>中国文艺才能更好地发展繁荣起来</u>。

TT：General Secretary Xi Jinping points out that <u>Chinese art can be better developed and become prosperous</u> only by adhering to innovation, learning the essence of the western paintings and blending it with Chinese art.

Analysis：In this example, the translator reversed the sentence order in translation because the typical English sentence order is subject+predicate+manner adverbial, which is

Chapter Six C-E Translation of Fine Art Commentary

contrary to the Chinese "只有……才" structure.

Example 2

ST：技术语言是绘画语言的基础,忽略技术语言,过分关注情节和主题,<u>是中国油画一个时期内的普遍现象</u>。这使得中国油画在很长时间里,以一种博物馆解说图、书籍彩色插图及宣传画的面貌出现。

TT：In a certain period, <u>it was a common phenomenon</u> to pay too much attention to stories and themes while neglecting techniques among Chinese painters. As a result, for a long time, the Chinese oil paintings took the forms of museum illustration chart, colorful illustrations of books and picture posters.

Analysis：In this example, the sentence which expresses the idea ("it was a common phenomenon") is preplaced before facts ("pay too much attention to stories and themes while neglecting techniques among Chinese painters") to cater to the English deductive way of expression, which is different from the Chinese inductive way of sentence construction in the ST.

6.4.7 Integrated translation method

Generally speaking, when long complicated Chinese sentences are translated, a comprehensive method is often adopted. Sometimes amplification, omission, division and combination are utilized together with the aim of generating a good version as illustrated in most examples above.

Example 1

ST：油画作者对此次考察的电视画面和摄影图片资料进行了细致研究,选取总书记与施齐文老夫妇亲切交谈的场景为主体,同时在创作中打破写实的限制,按自己的理解选取画面,截取总书记在得知老夫妇都不识字,家里又没有电视,所以老伴石爬专问他"怎么称呼您？"总书记笑答"我是人民的勤务员"后,亲切地握住64岁石大妈手说"你是大姐"的这一寓意深刻的瞬间,典型化地再现了总书记对扶贫地区人民群众的深切关爱。这一场面也成为他要求各级党委更精准扶贫的真实写照。

TT：The painter made detailed study on the television scenes and photographs about this inspection and selected the moment when the General Secretary Xi Jinping has a cordial conversation with Shi Qiwen and his wife. The painter broke the limitation of realistic painting during creation and chose the most meaningful moment as the topic. Since the Shis' are illiterate and have no television, they didn't recognize the General Secretary, the wife Shi Pa asked the General Secretary Xi Jinping "How can I address you?", Xi smiled and answered "I am people's servant" and then held Shi's hand kindly and said "You are my elder sister", which reflects General Secretary Xi's heartfelt affection to people in the poverty-stricken areas. This is also the real reflection of Xi's requirement to party committees at all levels to help to alleviate poverty with exact target.

Analysis: In this example, the method of "combination", "division" and "restructuring" are all employed to convey the communicative effect of the original text accurately and make the version smooth and idiomatic.

In summary, when Chinese are translated into English, we should consider many factors like culture differences, languages features, and the purpose of the ST and TT as well as TT readers' background knowledge about China and their expectations. Then different translation methods should be employed to achieve the communicative effect in the translation. For example, through smooth and successful translation of Professor Wang Haili's oil paintings, we intend to make the foreign viewers understand the content of the paintings and realize the heroic spirit and unconquerable traits of Chinese nation and army and convey to the world our determination to defend the peace and national dignity.

References

ANHOLT S, 2000. Another one bites the grass: making sense of international advertising [M]. New York: Wiley.

ARRANZ P, IGOR J. 2005. The discourse of British tourist promotion and its translation into Spanish[D]. Oviedo: Universidad de Oviedo.

BAKER M, 1992. In other words: a coursebook on translation[M]. London: Routledge.

BELL R T, 1991. Translation and translating: theory and practice[M]. London: Longman.

CHAO Y R, 1968. A grammar of spoken Chinese [M]. Los Angeles: University of California Press.

DELLA S, 2003. Longman advanced American dictionary[M]. Beijing: Foreign Language Teaching and Research Press.

FEDLER F, 1993. Reporting for the print media[M]. Orland: Harcourt Brace Jovanovich, Inc.

FOWLER R, 1991. Language in the news[M]. London: Routledge.

FRANCESCONI S, 2007. English for tourism promotion: Italy in British tourism texts [M]. Milano: Hoepli.

GENTZLER E, 2001. Contemporary translation theories[M]. 2nd ed. London: Routledge.

HORENBERG G H F, 2015. Tourism advertising: comparing the effects of push & pull factors in advertising[D]. Enschede: University of Twente.

JESPERSEN O, 1954. Language, its nature, development and origin[M]. London: George Allen & Unwin Ltd.

JOOS M, 1962. The five clocks[M]. Bloomington: Indiana University Press.

KEEBLE R, 1998. The newspapers handbook[M]. London: Routledge.

KELLY D, 1998. The translation of texts from the tourist sector: textual conventions, cultural distance and other constraints[J]. Trans: revista de traductología, (2): 33-42.

KOLLER W, 1995. The concept of equivalence and the object of translation studies[J]. Target,7: 191-222.

LI C N, THOMPSON S A, 1976. Subject and topic: a new typology[M]. New York: Academic Press.

MACI S M, 2007. Virtual touring: the web language of tourism[J]. Linguistica filologia,

25: 41-65.

MENCHER M, 2003. News reporting and writing[M]. Beijing: Tsing Hua University Press.

MENCHER M, 1994. News reporting and writing[M]. 6th ed. Lowa: Browner & Benchmark Publishers.

MENCHER M, 1996. Basic media writing[M]. Chicago: Brown & Benchmark Publishers.

MIDDLETON V, FYALL A, MORGAN M, et al., 2009. Marketing in travel and tourism [M]. 4th ed. London: Elsevier.

MUNDAY J, 2001. Introducing translation studies: theories and applications[M]. London: Routledge.

NARASHIMHA R, 1998. Style in journalism[M]. India: Oriented Longman Limited.

NEWMARK P, 1981. Approaches to translation[M]. 1st ed. Oxford: Pergamon Press.

NEWMARK P, 2001. A textbook of translation[M]. Shanghai: Shanghai Foreign Language Education Press.

NEWMARK P, 2006. About translation[M]. Beijing: Foreign Language Teaching and Research Press.

NIDA E A, 1964. Towards a science of translating[M]. Leiden: Brill.

NIDA E A, 1976. A framework for the analysis and evaluation of theories of translation[J]. Translation, application and research, (6):64.

NIDA E A, 1993. Language, culture and translating[M]. Shanghai: Shanghai Foreign Language Education Press.

NIDA E A, 1995. Dynamic equivalence in translating[M]//CHAN S, POLLARD D. An encyclopedia of translation. Hong Kong: The Chinese University of Hong Kong Press.

NIDA E A, TABER C R, 2004. The theory and practice of translation[M]. Shanghai: Shanghai Foreign Language Education Press.

NORD C, 1997. A functional typology of translation in Anna Trosborg (ed) scope and scopes in translation[M]. Amsterdam: Benjamins.

NORD C, 2001. Translating as a purposeful activity: functional approaches explained[M]. Shanghai: Shanghai Foreign Language Education Press, Manchester: St. Jerome Publishing.

NORD C, 2006. Text analysis in translation: theory, methodology, and didactic application of a model for translation-oriented text analysis[M]. Beijing: Foreign Language Teaching and Research Press.

PATTANAIK P, 1994. The art of translation[M]. New Delhi: Harman Publishing House.

QUIRK R S, 1985. The English language in a global context[M]//QUIRK R, WIDDOWSON H. English in the world: teaching and learning the language and literatures. Cambridge: Cambridge University Press: 1-6.

References

REISS K, 1971. The limitations and possibilities of translation criticism[M]. Munich: Hueber.

REISS K, HANS V, 1984. Grundlegung einer allgemeinen translationstheorie [M]. Tubigen: Niemeyer.

REISS K, 1989. Text types, translation types and translation assessment [M]// CHESTERMAN A. Readings in translation theory, Helsinki: Oy Finn Lectura Ab: 105-115.

REISS K, 2001. Translation criticism—the potentials & limitations[M]. Manchester: St. Jerome, Philadelphia: American Bible Society.

SANNING H, 2010. Lost and found in translating tourist texts: domesticating, foreignising or neutralising approach[J]. The journal of specialized translation, 13(2): 124-137.

SNELL-HORNBY M, 1987. Translation as a cross-cultural event: midnight's children-Midtternachtskinder[J]. Indian journal of applied linguistics, 13(2): 91-105.

SUMBERG C, 2004. Brand leadership at stake: selling France to British tourists[J]. The translator, 10(2): 329-353.

TORRESI I, 2010. Translating promotional and advertising texts[M]. Manchester: St. Jerome.

TROSBORG A, 2012. Text typology and translation[M]. Shanghai: Shanghai Foreign Language Education Press.

VALDEÓN R A, 2009. Info-promotional material discourse and its translation: the case of the Asturian tourist board texts[J]. Across languages and cultures, 10(1): 21-47.

VERMEER H J, 1978. Ein rahmen fur eine allegemeine translationstheorie[J]. Lebende Sprachen, 23(3): 99-102.

VERMEER H J, 1983. Translation theory and linguistics[M]//ROINILA, ORFANOS, CONDIT. Näkökohtia käänämisen tutki-muksesta. Joensuun: Joensuun korkeakoulu: 1-10.

VERMEER H J, 1987. What does it mean to translate? [J]. Indian journal of applied linguistics, 13(2): 25-33.

VERMEER H J, 1989a. Skopos und translationsauftrag—aufsatze [M]. Heidelberg: Universitat Heidelberg.

VERMEER H J, 1989b. Skopos and commission in translation action [M]// CHESTERMAN A. Readings in translation theory. Helsinki: Oy Finn Lectura Ab: 87-173.

VERMEER H J, 2001. A framework for a general theory of translation[M]. Shanghai: Shanghai Foreign Education Press.

WILSS W, 1993. English translation as translation science: problems and methods[M]. Tubingen: Narr.

陈刚,2004.旅游翻译与涉外导游[M].北京:中国对外翻译出版公司.
段云礼,2009.实用商务英语翻译[M].北京:对外经济贸易大学出版社.
贾文波,2004.应用翻译功能论[M].北京:中国对外翻译出版公司.
廖瑛,莫再树,2004.国际商务英语语言与翻译研究[M].北京:机械工业出版社.
连淑能,1993.英汉对比研究[M].北京:高等教育出版社.
连淑能,2000.英汉对比研究:增订本[M].北京:高等教育出版社.
刘其中,2004.新闻翻译教程[M].北京:中国人民学出大版社.
刘美岩,2010.对比语言学[M].西安:西北工业大学出版社.
潘红,2010.商务英语英汉翻译教程[M].北京:中国商务出版社.
熊兵,2012.应用翻译研究视角的嬗变(2000—2012)[J].中国翻译,(6):11-17.
许明武,2003.新闻英语与翻译[M].北京:中国对外翻译出版公司.
杨山青,2010.实用文体英汉翻译[M].北京:国防工业出版社.
张沉香,2008.功能目的理论与应用翻译研究[M].长沙:湖南师范大学出版社.
张美芳,2013.文本类型、翻译目的及翻译策略[J].上海翻译,(4):5-10.
张新红,李明,2003.商务英语翻译:英译汉[M].北京:高等教育出版社.
http://www.destination360.com/north-america/us/nevada/las-vegas#
http://www.bighonglcong.com/bhk-photo/loverstock-s
http://www.destination360.com/north-america/us/washington/seattle/space-needle
http://www.voanews.com
http://www.chinadaily.com.cn